A Disrupted History

A Disrupted History

The New Left and the New Capitalism

Greg Calvert & Carol Neiman

Random House New York

Book design by Paula Wiener

Library of Congress Catalog Card Number: 73–140695
ISBN: 0–394–46267–x

Manufactured in the United States of America
by H. Wolff Book Manufacturing Co.
3   5   7   9   8   6   4   2
FIRST EDITION

For the Jello Girl
    and the Lemon Light
    and Tim.
And for the time when
    we were all
One Body in Love.

Contents

Preface

An uneasiness which borders on despair accompanies the final
editing and rewriting of this book. It seems strange indeed to
submit the final draft of a work on radical social theory to a
large and important American publishing house which is part
of an even larger complex of corporate power within the total
context of America's industrial and military empire. It is not,
however, the simple question of the implications others might
draw from the place of publication: we faced that particular
contradiction two years ago when we first arrived in the august
offices of Random House with a partial manuscript that led
to a contract, an advance and, finally, to the work (and pro-
crastinations from work) which will find its way to the book-
stalls and perhaps to the hearts of readers. There are more
complex questionings abroad in the land of our not-yet-certain
souls.

Social theory can sometimes soar above the day-by-day struggles for a socialist and humanized world. That has never been
our particular talent, nor should we pretend such a stance
before our readers. Though as activists and writers our back-
grounds differ enormously—the one a working class man
turned for a time into the paths of bourgeois academia, the
other a working class woman turned from the beginning away
from the Ivy Halls toward movement activism—we have shared
the pain and frustration of the last two years. One of us has
been working most recently as a para-professional in a large
hospital. The other has been writing poetry and a novel. But
both have seen the disintegration of the organization (SDS)
which we helped to build and the repression of our former
friends and comrades. Precisely because the book presents an

analysis and program which is today foreign to most of the remnants of the American New Left, and because few of our former comrades regard it as a significant approach to the question of radical social change in this period, we feel that these arguments should re-enter the mainstream of radical thought and be discussed and transcended in the fashion of all relevant radical social theory. Not to denounce, but to go beyond inadequacies, should be the guiding practice of the left as it confronts its great theoretical debates. SDS did not have this practice. Rather it was thwarted and stifled by a dogmatic rigidity which killed debate before it had ever gotten off the ground. Somehow we failed to accept different perceptions as a basis for ongoing dialogue and chose instead the Old Left approach of the "correct line mentality" which excluded growth and the honest interchange of opposing views.

The experiences of SDS ought to be sobering for our poetic "community of the faithful" which began as a New Left and which ended in dogmatic posturing and programs which could not be implemented without an apocalytic revolutionary moment. We have not achieved one single radical reform which transferred power from the corporate elite to the people. The military posture of the Black Panther Party has produced many martyrs but not armed self-defense of the black community; the experiences of the 1960s, with all their pain and struggle, have not left one mass-based organization which has the power to resist either repression or co-optation; some of our friends are dead—too many; some of our friends are underground in a noble but spurious attempt to make classical terrorism the catalytic force for the creation of a viable revolutionary movement. We who tried most desperately to turn America-the-Obscene into America-the-Beautiful failed miserably and our brothers and sisters are dying as a result of that failure. It is not an easy atmosphere in which to publish a book.

In spite of it all, we still feel that an analysis which attempts to incorporate categories like "neocapitalism," "the new working class," and "the new contradictions" into the mainstream of radical thought in America is not irrelevant to the major tasks which face the remnants of the New Left in the 1970s. Nor does writing a novel or working in a hospital among para-professionals seem irrelevant. What does seem totally out of date and out of the realm of relevance is the assumption that critical thought ended with the translations of Lenin's works or the *Thoughts of Chairman Mao Tse-tung*, or even with the definitive editions of Sigmund Freud. Human questioning in radical terms continues despite the official oligarchies. The New Left still seems possible in spite of its temporary reversion to the form and content of the Old. Faith, although it is defined well as "the illogical belief in the improbable," still seems revolutionary. Death, however overwhelming in its temporary grip on life, seems conquerable. And, as always, new life is possible.

We wish to thank the Rabinowitz Foundation which gave us respite from many more months of penury to continue work on the book. We wish especially to thank Staughton Lynd and Alice Lynd, whose many suggestions saved this book from its worst flaws, and whose friendship helped save us from despair.

Greg Calvert
Carol Neiman Calvert

Dallas, August, 1970.

A Note on Language

Words are useful if they express what's really on your mind. The language of the Left—socialism, communism, anarchism—expresses moments of human experience which have been frozen into slogans and reduced to meaninglessness.

We have worried a lot about the problem of language and the way in which it became a problem for the New Left. We never really resolved the problem satisfactorily and adopted "libertarian socialist" to describe what we felt at least sounded best. Then, one day recently, we asked a musician friend of ours what he thought people in the good society would call it. Would they say this is anarchy, or this is communism, or this is socialism? "No," Tom Rossen replied, "I think that perhaps they would simply say: *This is a society of friends.*"

Being hung-up on a noun reveals an identity problem. When I use the phrase: I am a ——— (Texan or American, or socialist or anarchist or communist), I express an uncomfortableness with simply being myself. Tom Rossen added another insight to the discussion. He said, "The only noun which I wish ever to describe me, the only way I want to be identified, is to say: *I am a lover.*"

That language seems comfortable. If you want to know what we mean by the good society, it is this. We would like to live in a world in which each person in the community of human-kind would have the deep and powerful experience of being in touch with his feelings and with himself, a community in which each individual could say: *"I am a lover in a society of friends."*

PART ONE

———

Theory and the New Left

1

Is There a New Left?

The American political scene at the beginning of the 1970s presents a strange set of historical contradictions strikingly different, at least on the surface, from the springtime of 1968 when the quadrennial electoral spectacle was last set in motion. Lyndon Johnson had just resigned; Martin Luther King was dead of an assassin's bullet; and America's black ghettos rose in an unprecedented wave of revolt. Two things seemed clear. First, the liberal Eastern wing of the ruling establishment would return to power through the candidacy of a Kennedy or a Rockefeller with the goal of re-establishing the policies of corporate liberalism and the welfare state which had been the formula for governing the neocapitalist social order since the 1930s. The war which LBJ had transformed from an adventure in pacification into a full-scale imperialist crusade would be liquidated as any sensible Wall Street banker would liquidate an obviously disastrous investment. The power of the military-industrial complex which Johnson had re-enforced to the advantage of the Southwest's armaments industries would be curbed.

At home, reform measures would divert and co-opt the growing forces of radicalism among the black and brown minorities and on the campuses. The course of liberal rule in the age of the New Capitalism, temporarily interrupted by the Johnson usurpation, would be played out in the managed and programmed pseudo-rationality which had characterized public life in the period prior to the Gulf of Tonkin Resolution.

Secondly, the growth of the New Left would resume the slower, more experimental character which had been its life-rhythm in the years before the bombing of North Vietnam. Its historical future seemed clear. Slowly but inevitably, as corporate liberalism would run out of bureaucratic solutions to the domestic problems of advanced industrial society, the perspectives of radicalism in the style of participatory democracy would win more adherents as the only logical alternative. Radicals could look forward to long term organizing projects among off-campus political constituencies. Parallel institutions and participatory democracy (or, maybe, to advance the rhetoric one step further, "participatory socialism") would once again rule as strategic concepts and daily practice within the New Left. SDS would slowly but surely become a mass-based campus organization: a radical union representing the majority of America's seven million students and providing a powerful lever for radical political change.

But circumstance disrupted the logic of history, precluding this sane and comprehensible dialectics for the 1970s. The spell of liberal magic surrounding the Kennedy clan was broken once again by the specter of political assassination. The emergence of George Wallace as a leader of a new right-wing movement with important grassroots support among blue-collar workers revealed that the liberal-labor alliance so carefully constructed by FDR was in a bad state of disrepair—if not on the verge of total disintegration. The labor bureaucrats could no longer deliver the votes of their dues paying constituency to the liberal politicians. And, as if liberalism's grasp on power in the country were not already sufficiently tenuous, the Chicago Convention in August revealed that the Democratic Party was bankrupt as the historical agent of liberal reform. Both through the events on the convention floor and the confrontations—with a John Connally ordering the votes and a Richard Daley ordering the cops—the election of Richard Nixon and his Agnew was assured. The "whole world" was indeed watching. And watch it should have, because the fate of humanity was being decided by a handful of corrupt politicians who claimed as their heritage the "New Deal"—neocapitalism's finest hour.

Two years later the *Vietnam* War became the War in Indochina. Students fell before the bullets of National Guardsmen on campuses. The Black Panther Party emerged in the ghettos and was brutally repressed. Law and order prevails—a politics of neo-conservatism in America—a politics of neo-Stalinism in Prague. Nowhere does the New Left, which once flourished in every advanced capitalist nation, exist as a real force. SDS has disintegrated, and where a mass radical organization once tried to organize towards a radical alternative, there now lie only broken fragments and the underground terrorist organization, Weathermen. The latter adopted as their slogan, "You don't need a Weatherman to know which way the wind blows." But one is forced to ask how we got blown so far off course in the storm, or if we can ever expect to find our way again.

Faced with the unexpected in history, the remnants of the New Left now ask themselves whether the phenomenon with which they identified was more than a utopian fantasy of the 1960s—a temporary historical aberration— or whether their movement will re-emerge from its current disarray to do meaningful battle on the stage of history. Clearly the fate of the New Left is bound to the fate of the Vietnamese revolutionaries. If the war is not ended, if Nixon does not withdraw and thus accept the reality of military defeat, then the scenario for freedom fighters in Southeast Asia is bleak. There is only one way the war can be "won" by United States forces: by resorting to the thermonuclear destruction of a major portion of Indochina and the genocidal destruction of the vast majority of the people of Vietnam, Cambodia and Laos. In that case, the domestic scenario for American society would also be written in the starkest of terms; total repression of all political dissent, the probable establishment of a military dictatorship, and the institution of a full-fledged American fascism. ("Good night, David; Good night, Chet; Goodbye, World.")

If that is the historical direction of our time, then the option chosen by the Weathermen makes sense for radicals. Not because they would thereby achieve the objective of revolutionary change, but because clandestinity or flight beyond the borders would remain the only possibilities for physical survival. Those who believe that fascism would provide a better chance for revolution ought to look more closely at the history of Germany and Italy in the 1920s—hardly a period replete with socialist victories. When Marx posed "socialism or barbarism" as the historical alternatives to modern capitalist civilization, he saw them as absolutes: he did not mean that socialism could ever grow out of barbarism. He realized that barbarism might simply beget more barbarism.

The current phase of conservatism and reaction in American politics appears as a disruption of the history of both liberalism and radicalism. How and why that disruption occurred is a subject of deep concern for both liberals and radicals. Whether it represents a temporary deviation or a new historical direction of long range significance is a question of primary importance for all of humankind.

While the New Left had failed to grasp the strategic opening presented by the collapse of the liberal-labor coalition of the New Deal era, the governing clique of the Nixon administration has clearly seized the time with a strategy for a new conservative coalition. That coalition is described by Kevin Phillips, a chief strategist in Attorney General John Mitchell's brain trust, in his book *The Emerging Republican Majority*, (Arlington House, New York, 1969). Phillips recognizes two fundamental facts which form the basis of the Republican strategy. First, the center of ruling class economic power has shifted from the Eastern establishment and Wall Street to the new industrialists of the South and Southwest with their brokers now seated in the Pentagon rather than in New York. Secondly, an electoral base—which could provide popular electoral support for a new conservative coalition —exists in the suburban strata which have emerged since World War II as an unorganized social force. In Kevin Phillips' own words:

"A new suburbia is being built across America by many millions of blue-collar and middle-level white-collar families in their twenties and thirties. This is the new young America on the move and from Southern California to Richmond, Virginia, to Long Island's Suffolk County, the movement is conservative."

It is the clearly stated intention of the new Republican Coalition to weld together this social force under the hegemony of the South-Southwest military-industrial complex on the basis of a reactionary political ideology.

The possibility also exists that the New Left can regroup

and seize the time for other ends around a program of liberation and people's control of their lives—a strategy of libertarian socialism based on community and working people's control. This book attempts to analyze many of the same social forces which Kevin Phillips perceives as a "white noose." Just as in the Great Depression of the 1930s a shift in ruling class coalitions offered an opening to both the left and the right, our own period offers the same challenge. The New Left must either rise from its ashes or get the romanticism out of its head if it is to meet this challenge.

This book is not primarily concerned with the rise of the new conservatism. Rather, its aim is to raise certain questions relating specifically to the interrupted history of the New Left—to interpret a social process whose political manifestations are temporarily obscured—in order to understand better the past failures and future possibilities. The wave of political reaction which has threatened to engulf the left since 1968 has certainly not been broken, and, although it only hovers in the wings of this study, the immediate concerns it generates occupy a stage front position in the minds of the authors. However, only a larger historical and theoretical context can begin to light the way beyond the impasse we face. Without such a context there can be no effective response to the politics of silent majoritarianism and its corollary—the repression of the left.

Neither the escalation of revolutionary rhetoric nor the multiplication of militant tactics will answer the hard questions which the social complexity of the advanced capitalist world poses. The discussion in the following pages traces the evolution of a set of categories—neocapitalism, new working class, and post-scarcity—and their implications for the possibility of realizing radical structural change in the advanced capitalist world. The second part of the book approaches the question of political practice and is placed in a strongly libertarian and decentralist framework. The libertarian conviction grows out of an experience of the disastrous effects which Leninist practice and authoritarian socialist forms produced within the context of SDS. But it relates also to the historical possiblity of—the necessity for—decentralization as an integral part of the *process* of radical political transformation.

A brief historical resumé of the experience of the New Left in the 1960s will help to situate the context in which the categories of analysis with which we will be dealing arose.

THE NEW LEFT AND THE
OLD IDEOLOGIES

It is a major error to assume that the New Left sprang full-blown from a carefully thought-out set of theoretical presuppositions. In fact, the contrary tended to be the general rule: namely, that young political activists began to seek out alternatives to the situations confronting them, in spite of the fact that they had no theoretical answers to the problem of social change in advanced capitalist society, and no ultimate political directions. Political activity (to use the language of the preamble to the Constitution of Students for a Democratic Society) was seen as a process of "bringing people out of isolation into community." It was understood that modern capitalism had left individuals powerless and isolated. The alternative was named: "building community" among powerless people.

Whatever clarity of political perspectives has developed within the New Left is largely the product of the day-to-day experience of political work. Slowly, and sometimes clumsily, New Leftists developed new answers and new approaches. In the process, the classics of the left were reexamined, redissected, and reinterpreted—without, it must be added, much help or encouragement from the Leninist cults of the past.

New Left activists began by building their politics out of their instincts, their "gut-level" reactions, their search for community, and their hope. Few of those who faced violence on the picket lines or who risked death in the Southern civil rights projects could have explained how their work would ultimately change America. More likely they would have been able to explain how it had changed their own lives. Their political work was often an act of faith. But the profound conviction remained that getting "involved" was the only answer to becoming a different kind of human being.

If any one subject of discussion has dominated the dialogues of the New Left, it is the question of identity. The question is not abstract but historical. Who are we? Anarchist or socialist? Marxist or existentialist? The charge often made against the New Left of mindless activism ("rebels without a program") has had a certain justification, but it also misses the point. Despite the lack of theory and the confused search for identity, there has been a deep conviction that the *personal* and the *political* could not be divorced; that the search for individual liberation must inevitably lead to public collective activity—to radical politics.

There was a story once told by New Left activists to illustrate their concept of the relationship between personal concerns and political struggle. Whether it is true, whether it is an accurate account of guerrilla methods in Guatemala, it is a valid interpretation of the dynamics of New Left organizing in the United States:

> It is said that when the Guatemalan guerrillas enter a new village they do not talk about the "anti-imperialist struggle,"

nor do they give lessons on dialectical materialism; neither do they distribute copies of the *Communist Manifesto* or of Chairman Mao's *On Contradiction*. Rather, they bring together the people in the center of the village and then, one by one, the guerrillas rise and talk about their own lives, about how they see themselves and how they came to be who they are, about their deepest longings and the things they have striven for and hoped for, about the way in which their deepest longings were frustrated by the society in which they lived.

Then the guerrillas encourage the villagers to talk about their own lives in the same way, and a marvellous thing begins to happen. People who thought that their deepest problems and frustrations were individual and personal discover that their problems and longings are all the same—that no one man is any different than the others. That, in Sartre's phrase, "in each man, there is all of man." And, finally, out of the discovery of their common humanity comes the decision that they must unite together in the struggle to destroy the conditions of their common oppression.[1]

THE FAILURE OF THE OLD IDEOLOGIES

The New Left grew out of the new conditions of post-World War II America—the affluent society, the lonely crowd, the silent generation of the 1950s—and there was no political vocabulary which could express or analyze its nature. Long before the New Left took form it had its prophetic forerunners in the Beat Generation—poets crying out against "America The Obscene" and the ugly meaninglessness of a society whose highest achievements were the Bomb and Disneyland. No one thought of this prophetic negation of America as "political," no one thought of the long-range *political* implications of the cultural revolt. "Politics" was something that took place around the ballot box every two or four years, and politicians were just another loathsome symptom of the undiagnosed disease which festered at the heart of the society.

The deeply political relevance of beat poetry was unnoticed because the poetry did not fit into the two existing political vocabularies. Neither the dominant ideology of liberalism nor the vulgar mechanistic Marxism of the Old Left could offer a political explanation or socioeconomic analysis of such seemingly vague and elusive phenomena as *alienation* and *meaninglessness*. The liberal world view argued that America was becoming an increasingly affluent, classless, and humane society where the revolutionary conflict of an earlier age had been successfully transcended, and all that was needed was a little patching-up from time to time—a little more welfare, a few more "rights," and more rigorous government regulation. The only enemies were the communists within, who refused to play by the rules of the liberal game, and the communists without, who were totalitarian conspirators dedicated to the destruction of all human values, almost in the same category as the Nazis. Liberal anticommunism justified the Cold War on the grounds of necessity while decrying its effects, nuclear armaments, as dangerous but remediable.

The Old Left, the Communist Party, and the Trotskyites, continued to declaim the now-hollow slogans of the 1930s.[2] They argued, quite correctly, that America continued to be a society structured by class, governed by those who had the power to make the important choices. The Old Left also reiterated its conviction that the industrial working class was *the* revolutionary force which would unite to overthrow the capitalist system. And because of this, only the most romantic or most nostalgic listeners responded to these analyses with acts of intellectual faith.

Neither the ideology of liberalism nor the Old Left's version of Marxism could deal adequately with the rising voices of a new generation whose critique of the society described it as "sick" and "obscene."

THE NEW ACTIVISM

The debate over the old ideologies became irrelevant as soon as political involvement through direct action became possible. The sterile and academic arguments of the 1950s were replaced by the direct confrontations of the 1960s. The silent generation of the 1950s, with its handful of outraged poets and prophets, gave way to the activist generation of the 1960s with tens, hundreds, thousands, and finally tens of thousands of young people putting America to the test by putting their bodies on the line in the new wave of confrontation politics. New organizations were formed, whose names clashed strangely with the traditional jargon of left wing politics—the Student Nonviolent Coordinating Committee (SNCC) and Students for a Democratic Society (SDS). It was this new activism which finally broke the liberal consensus, and with these first cracks in the ideological iron curtain of liberalism enough light entered to reveal that political truth must lie beyond. Out of this concrete experience of political struggle, the New Left began to emerge, to grow, and to fill the political void with a wealth of new data out of which its own analysis and its own theoretical perspective might emerge. There was no other way to learn because there was no better political mentor than the direct experience of American reality and American power.

Two issues were central in shaping the political consciousness of the new movement: civil rights and the Vietnam War. Both these issues first developed as essentially liberal ones and fell easily into a liberal program for correcting errors and patching up holes in what liberalism regarded as an essentially sound system. But out of the concrete experience of the civil rights and antiwar movements grew a new perception of the meaning of those issues and of their rootedness in the most fundamental dynamics of American capitalism. This was the process of "radicalization," of discovering the roots, which young people in the movement constantly referred to and which pointed to the realization that racism and imperialism—the inevitable twin offspring of capitalist domination and exploitation—could only be fought in the context of a long-term perspective for the revolutionary transformation of America.

Everywhere the movement organized and struggled, the liberal consensus and world view suffered more exposure and more defeats. In the civil rights movement, the deep contradiction between the rhetoric of American freedom and the reality of American oppression was laid bare. In the antiwar movement, the liberal assumption that power in America would yield to the force of moral suasion was tested and destroyed. Marx had argued that "No social order ever disappears before all the productive forces for which there is room in it have developed." The first lesson of the New Left seemed to be that *no ideology ever perishes before all the basic assumptions which it contains have been tested in real experience.*

Although the new radical activists were far from developing an analysis and strategy, they had broken through the political inertia of the society. The outrage of the Beat Generation poets was finding its political vocabulary in the growth of the New Left. Racism and imperialism were the issues which gave political form to the generation's deep emotions and convictions.

But the New Left's sense of the integrative nature of these issues was the basis for the qualitatively new character of its commitment. War and racism were not flaws in an otherwise perfect system, as the liberals believed. These conditions could not be eradicated by a change in management or economic structure. Rather, the Vietnam war and the oppression of black people were symptomatic of an entire system of values and relationships which thwarted and perverted human potential. The only way out of the trap of domination and exploitation, the New Left believed, was to discover new values, new sets of relationships, in a community which allowed each of its members freedom of expression and development. This commitment made it impossible to stand outside the world and dictate abstract "answers" to abstract "problems." The New Left summed up its profound differences with the Old Left and liberalism by declaring that "the revolution is about 6ur lives."

RADICAL CONSCIOUSNESS: NEGATION AND SELF-AFFIRMATION

The success of liberalism as both the dominant world view and political practice of advanced capitalist societies depends on the ability of existing institutions to provide a sufficiently comfortable and stable environment so that a smooth running sociopolitical process does not threaten the existing economic order. Ultimately, liberalism rests on its ability to privatize existence and to convince the public that any unsolved problems are "personal" problems. Thus the controls on which the social order rests are in large part internalized.

The practical political results of liberal domination are twofold. First, individuals are no longer able to identify the sociopolitical enemy as exterior to their own being. Secondly, because the source of conflict is "within the individual," public political activities assume the forms of penance or missionary ventures designed to expiate guilt. Because the internalization of the repressive social order has made it impossible to distinguish between the self and society the liberal sees his political acts as public service. Unlike the liberal, the radical experiences his political acts as part of a movement of collective self-affirmation which seeks to bring into being a new person and a new society. The absence of the dynamic of social negation and self-affirmation clearly distinguishes liberalism and liberal reformism from radical and revolutionary movements.

The important point must be emphasized in elaborating the difference between radical or revolutionary consciousness and liberal-reformist consciousness. The profound gap which separates a liberal reform movement from a revolutionary movement is revealed in the dynamics of its participants.

Radical consciousness among youth in the new movements of the 1960s has generally emerged first as "anti-system consciousness"—that is, as a non-historical, non-socialist rejection of the dominant social institutions. This form of consciousness is based on a deep sense of alienation from and rejection of the entire structure of demands and alternatives which are imposed and offered by an advanced capitalist society. On the other hand, the capitalist system is neither identified as the specific mode of exploitation and oppression nor as the specific source of that exploitation and oppression. Thus we see rock festivals emerge as an important cultural form in the late 1960s. But while many positive values are incorporated in the Woodstock Nation, those values do not incorporate a conscious demand for self-determination nor an explicit opposition to capitalist control. Entrepreneurial "producers" make enormous profits from ticket sales. Rock bands perform from a stage and thus reenact the practice of rule-by-spectacle that characterizes the larger society.

The revolt against the repressive forms of the dominant society and the nascent affirmation of a new selfhood in the youth revolt is undoubtedly the most important cultural phenomenon of the 1960s. Despite its low level of political articulation, it brings an entirely new element to radical social criticism: *the critique of the programmed society.* But there too lies its internal contradiction. It grasps the totality of social oppression at an instinctual level but fails to identify the structural and historical sources of that oppression at the intellectual level. This separation of feeling and intellect reproduces social schizophrenia by inversion and leaves the youth cultural revolt prey to those who are powerful enough and clever enough to understand the manipulation of instinct. Frightening parallels can be drawn between the rock spectacle and rule-by-spectacle in Nazi Germany. Such notions are neither definitive nor adequate; but they provide a necessary anecdote to the naïve notion that rock culture is the perfect embodiment of the good society.

The negation of dominant institutions and the radical affirmation of self, contained however imperfectly in the antisystem youth movements, have been the basis of a major onslaught on dominant ideology. The inability of both liberals and the Old Left to respond creatively to this new social development reveals more clearly than anything else the bankruptcy of their positions. Neither has been able to subsume the fundamental New Left demands. All that the politics of liberalism has been able to offer is more missionary activity and more self-abnegation.

BEYOND THE POLITICS OF GUILT

The political response of liberal guilt received its first direct challenge from the black movement. In their search for a political movement which would give meaningful expression to their sense of alienation, college students—

both black and white—had gone South to join the struggle for civil rights. The search for a political identity eventually led black and white students into a head-on clash—a clash which eventually produced the Black Power position, elaborated by SNCC in 1965–66. Black Power reflected a variety of tensions in the black wing of the movement, including the opposition to the tactics of nonviolence which had been imposed by the liberal-reformist Southern Christian Leadership Conference (SCLC). Despite its ambiguities, Black Power was generally accepted by both black and white activists as a positive development.

Of central importance in the new position was the notion of black consciousness. Prior liberal integration programs had always inhibited the development of a radical rejection of the dominant society and, as such, had reinforced the guilt and self-hatred of black people. Black consciousness was an articulated negation of the dominant society and an affirmation of the selfhood of black people. "Black is beautiful" became the proud slogan of the awakening consciousness of militant elements in the black community. However, despite the presence of black militants with a revolutionary anticapitalist perspective within the Black Power movement, the slogan itself did not present the anticapitalist position of a class analysis. Increasingly, Black Power came to represent a cultural black nationalism with separatist aspirations. Even political demands like "black control of black communities" were fundamentally ambiguous; for black control could easily mean black bourgeois or petit-bourgeois control.

Black consciousness was an important but nevertheless insufficient basis for the development of a revolutionary political perspective. At the same time, however, the Black Power movement played a crucial role in precipitating the development of a radical perspective and in destroying the remnants of liberalism within the New Left. When black organizations implemented their demand for organizational self-control, they told the whites to go home and organize in their own communities. The trauma among white student activists was severe but the results were, in the long run, healthy; for it forced the New Left to reexamine its roots and to develop a perspective for political organizing within the conditions which had produced a white student movement in the first place. It was harder to play the liberal game of constituency-hunting in order to avoid coming to terms with one's roots and one's life.

Although some white activists did get involved in northern ghetto organizing (for instance, the Economic Research and Action Project of SDS), the shift of student activism was generally back toward the campus. The Berkeley confrontation of 1964 provided the backdrop while the issue of the war in Vietnam provided the new focus. (SDS called the first national protest march against the war, which took place on April 17, 1965.) For many off-campus constituencies, the antiwar movement remained another liberal protest movement. Not so for the New Left on the campuses; there the issue of the war soon became an issue of university involvement in the war, and with this development the latent question of the relation of students to the larger society was raised in a highly political atmosphere.

Among other issues related to the war, resistance to the draft became one of the most important focuses of radical organizing. The draft resistance movement involved a broad spectrum of motivations and beliefs, but it brought to the New Left a new understanding of the objective social position of students in the society. This understanding grew out of a confrontation with and analysis of the II–S draft deferment for college students. Radical students had always suffered qualms of conscience concerning what seemed to be a privileged position regarding military service. It was only when they began to understand the repressive manipulative function of the II–S itself that their guilt was replaced by a deeper consciousness of the conditions of their own oppression in the society. In the January 20, 1967, issue of *New Left Notes*[3] appeared an article by Peter Henig, entitled, "On The Manpower Channelers." Henig set out to demonstrate that the Selective Service System was designed to have much broader ramifications than simply providing conscripts for the military. Its function was to effect "manpower channeling" or "manpower flow" in a way which would directly influence the life decisions of all young men in the society. In particular, the system of college deferments was designed to channel young men into the multiversity where they would be trained for the millions of new scientific, professional, and technical jobs created by the new technology. Henig quoted from an article called "Channeling" in the *Selective Service Orientation Kit:*

> Delivery of manpower for induction, the process of providing a few thousand men with transportation to a reception center, is not much of an administrative or financial challenge. *It is in dealing with the other millions of registrants that the System is heavily occupied, developing more effective human beings in the national interest.* [Emphasis added by Henig]

The SSO document applauded the effectiveness of its system of coercion in the following words:

> Educators, scientists, engineers, and their professional organizations, during the last ten years particularly, have been

convincing the American public that for the mentally quali-
fied man there is a special order of patriotism other than service in uniform—that for the man having the capacity, dedicated service as a civilian in such fields as engineering, the
sciences, and teaching constitute the ultimate in their expression of patriotism. A large segment of the American public has been convinced that this is true.

It is in this atmosphere that the young man registers at age
eighteen and pressures begin to force his choice. He does not
have the inhibitions that a philosophy of universal service in
uniform would engender. The door is open for him as a student to qualify if capable in a skill badly needed by his nation. He has many choices and is prodded to make a decision.

The psychological effect of this circumstantial climate depends upon the individual, his sense of good citizenship,
his love of country and its way of life. He can obtain a sense
of well-being and satisfaction that he is doing as a civilian
what will help his country most. This process encourages
him to put forth his best effort and removes to some degree
the stigma that has been attached to being out of uniform.

In the less patriotic and more selfish individual it engenders a sense of fear, uncertainty, and dissatisfaction which
motivates him, nevertheless, in the same direction. He com-
plains of the uncertainty which he must endure; he would
like to be able to do as he pleases; he would appreciate a
certain future with no prospect of military service or civilian
contribution, but he complies with the needs of the national
health, safety, or interest—or is denied deferment.

Throughout his career as a student, the pressure—the
threat of loss of deferment—continues. It continues with
equal intensity after graduation. His local board requires
periodic reports to find out what he is up to. He is impelled
to pursue his skill rather than embark upon some less important enterprise and is encouraged to apply his skill in an
essential activity in the national interest. The loss of deferred
status is the consequence for the individual who acquired

the skill and either does not use it or uses it in a nonessential activity.

The psychology of granting wide choice under pressure to take action is the American or indirect way of achieving what is done by direction in foreign countries where choice is not permitted.

Henig's article was key in breaking through the veil of false consciousness regarding the situation of students and the nature of the university. Following it, came a lively discussion and a series of theoretical papers. The first, "Towards a Theory of Social Change," was presented by its authors in resumé form at an SDS educational conference at Princeton in February of 1967.[4] It was followed that spring by a pamphlet, "The Multiversity: Crucible of the New Working Class," [5] written by Carl Davidson, then National Vice President of SDS. Together these papers presented an analysis of students and the multiversity which broke sharply with past American left-wing interpretations.

Essentially the new viewpoint argued that the traditional analysis of students as petit-bourgeois intelligentsia was incorrect. Since the Second World War the American university had been transformed into the multiversity. It was no longer an institution which trained a narrow stratum of "middle-class professionals and gave a facade of culture to the sons of the ruling class. The needs of the new technology had forced the transformation of the old liberal arts institution into a new kind of institution which had as its primary task the training of scientific, technical, and professional workers to fill the labor needs of advanced industrial capitalism. Furthermore, it was understood that modern capitalist technology had necessitated the long-range transformation of the total labor force from the blue-collar worker on the line to the technician and engineer and scientist who would design and run the automated and cybernated machinery of the new era of computerized production. There was a long-range shift from the "old working class" to the "new working class" at the level of production itself. The multiversity was the primary social instrument of this transformation.[6]

Suddenly, it became clear that the implications of a New Left student movement for an advanced industrial society could be drawn in terms of the basic economic processes which were at work. First, it linked the growth of the new student life style and the student movement to fundamental industrial-economic trends. Secondly, it destroyed the liberal image of the university as an "Ivory Tower" which stood aloof from the demands of the workaday world. Thirdly, it provided a coherent picture of where students (and particularly student radicals) would be once they graduated from a purely student movement—in the institutions of production, socialization, and social control beyond the campus. Seven million students in the American system of higher education were no longer an isolated phenomenon but rather a part of a fundamental process of social transformation.

Other questions were raised which were more difficult to answer. How should university-trained workers be reached and organized beyond the campus? What would be the political relationship between university-trained workers and other strata of the working class—and between them and the poor and unemployed? These questions and many others remained unanswered, but a vital new breakthrough in the area of "class analysis" and modern industrial society had been made.

It was at this point that the theoretical development of the New Left clashed directly with the ideological position of the Old Left. According to existent "Marxist" analysis, the industrial working class was *the* revolutionary stratum of society. Students were part of the "middle class" or petite bourgeoisie, or perhaps belonged to the "intelligentsia." They were, therefore, a privileged stratum in society and not to be regarded as a potential revolutionary constituency in their own right. Their task, or rather the task of those few who would renounce their class privilege, was, according to this Old Left position, to devote their energies to organizing among industrial workers, the *real* proletariat.

Not only did this Old Left viewpoint ignore the fundamental alterations in class structure and work which had been transforming the nature of the labor force for a generation, it demanded that students see themselves as mere adjuncts to other movements. This time the politics of guilt and missionary activity were not to be directed at the black community but rather in the direction of industrial workers. Not only was the Old Left blind to the real role of the multiversity in the transformation of the labor force and the training of a new and vitally important sector of the work force to fit the needs of the new technology, but it was attempting to enforce false consciousness within one group in the society—a group which was beginning to develop a revolutionary class consciousness of its relationship to the means of production. Old Left ideological categories centering on "the industrial working class" hindered rather than aided the development of socialist consciousness among students. In calling students "middle class," the Old Left was promoting a false picture of class relations in the society—a false picture which was precisely the same as that promoted by the governing ideology.

In the words of a former National Secretary of SDS, Michael Spiegel, the problem could be posed as follows:[7]

> Our perception of ourselves within a class analysis, or of students as a whole within a class analysis, has presented us with some difficulty. We are faced with the definition which

the ruling class has provided for us—we are supposed to be members of the elite in this society, being educated to take over the "positions of leadership." A consciousness which defines students as members of the elite is obviously destructive not only to the establishment of our own identity as radicals, but also to our ability to become a vehicle for the challenging of ruling class values. We cannot see ourselves building a totally déclassé movement of people who stand outside of the classes of society as pure revolutionaries. One may be able to build a cadre who perceive themselves in that way, but not a mass movement. A mass movement must grow out of the experiences and oppression of people's lives. An organization must see itself as being able to speak for a group of people out of a set of values, but to accept the false definition of the role of students in this society denies us the ability to build anything more than a small organization of guilty, alienated youth who see themselves as "denying class privilege" (an unheard-of basis for building a mass movement).

A class is defined by its relationship to the means of production; by whether or not it controls those means and has the power to direct their course. As students, it would be difficult to say that we are the oppressed—but our class situation is certainly not one of control over the means of production (or of eventual control over them)—at least this is true for the vast majority of students. Thus our interests lie with others who have the same relationship to the means of production (for most of them, their material condition is also much worse than students—they are more clearly "oppressed.") The values of a student struggle must be seen as part of a broader class struggle against the ruling class. (Even though the other elements of the struggle may not have emerged yet, the values must show implicit support of other potential struggles.)

A correct understanding of our own consciousness in these terms makes it possible for us to not only "fight our own battles," but also to link up with other groups of oppressed people (in determining values, conscious strategy, and direction, if not in tactical or strategic coalition.) If we are to direct our struggle against the oppression of all people, we must first be clear about our own relationship to the class structure of America. No organization ever succeeded in building a strong movement for social change out of guilt—by building the consciousness of a movement on the motivation that one is in fact a member of the class of the oppressors and must salve that guilt. If we are to go beyond the politics of alienation, we must be able to present students with an analysis which does not motivate them to move out of guilt produced by false consciousness. In this respect, the widespread use of the concept of manpower channelling when working with draft resistance has been very important. There is some form of manpower channelling in all ordered societies. It can be democratic or autocratic. Manpower channelling is no replacement for a class analysis, but it can open the way for a legitimate class analysis by destroying the self-concept in middle class students that they are members of the ruling class and that their interests are thus tied to that class. In fact, manpower channelling shows how students are manipulated like everyone else.

FROM PROTEST TO RESISTANCE

The antiwar movement which developed to protest American aggression in Vietnam had several important and yet ambiguous effects on the development of the New Left. It led to a deeper questioning and understanding of American capitalism by exposing the nature of American economic and political imperialism abroad. At the same time, it led to considerable confusion concerning the effect of that imperialism on our own struggle within the advanced neocapitalist world. Perhaps its most disorienting consequence was the development of a romantic identification with the spirit and heroes of guerrilla warfare in the Third

World. Because of the exciting accomplishments of the Vietnamese, Chinese, and Cuban struggles, and, because of the difficulties of imagining a successful revolutionary movement in the advanced capitalist world, young New Leftists came to regard these movements as identical with their own. This mistaken and naïve perception—the failure to recognize the enormous differences between the conditions for revolutionary movements for national liberation in the Third World and those of an advanced industrial society—remains at the core of much of the factional disputes which currently rage in the New Left.

At its most superficial level, this misunderstanding leads to the assumption that some adaptation of the strategy and methods of guerrilla struggle can be developed for our own society. In many cases, there is a failure to recognize that the purpose of guerrilla insurrection is not to seize power on the spot but to inspire the frightened or apathetic peasant population and encourage them in the belief that the struggle can be waged, that the fight offers a real hope of victory. At a more sophisticated level, it leads to an adoption of the world revolutionary perspective of the Chinese Communist Party—the perspective of Maoism. According to this viewpoint, it is the successful waging of anti-imperialist struggles for national liberation which will eventually erode the power of the capitalist "metropolis" (including the Soviet Union) and finally reawaken the revolutionary consciousness of the industrial workers in the advanced industrial world.

A more realistic tendency in response to the phenomenon of America's aggression in Vietnam was the draft resistance movement. Often beginning as nonpolitical pacifism, but quickly developing into a politically articulate movement, draft resistance became one of the most vital areas of New Left organizing. The draft resistance position had historical precedent in the student-led opposition to the Algerian War in France. While the Stalinist French Communist Party refused to recognize draft resistance as a legitimate position, young people in France went outside the existing framework of left wing politics and organized their own movement under the name of Young Resistance (*Jeune Résistance*).[8] Using the rhetoric of the French movement but applying to it an analysis of the specific functioning of the draft in American society (channelling), young draft resisters contributed significantly to the radicalization of the whole antiwar movement. The high point of this development came with the October 21, 1967 march on the Pentagon under the slogan "From Dissent to Resistance." Tens of thousands of young people swarmed all over the giant cathedral of American imperialism, burned their draft cards, held a teach-in for the assembled troops, and encouraged soldiers to desert with chants of *Join Us!*

Internationally, draft resistance and its corollary, the encouragement of desertion, brought the American New Left into significant contact for the first time with its European counterparts. Groups like the German SDS actively undertook programs of support for American GI's wishing to desert from their NATO bases in order to avoid being sent to Vietnam. Both draft resistance and desertion continued to be a major thorn in the side of a government which cannot wage unpopular wars without conscription. More and more, the resistance movement began to see its goal as undermining the ability of the war makers to continue their aggressive posture by robbing them of their human resources. Back on the campuses, resistance strategies developed around the relationship of the university to the needs and goals of American imperialism and militarism. A host of targets were uncovered, ranging from military recruiters to chemical-biological warfare research projects. The most spectacular protest against the "imperialist uses of the university" was the Columbia University rebellion of the spring of 1968. At Columbia, the primary target of the demand was the Institute for Defense Analysis (IDA) with which the university had important and highly secret ties. The second demand of the students—stoppage of the construction of the Morningside Heights gymnasium—built a link with the black community in Harlem, which is exploited and pushed around as a real estate enterprise by Columbia. Students argued that the battle which they were waging against IDA and the struggle of black people for self-determination in Harlem were part and parcel of the same anti-imperialist movement. At the same time, the argument that black people were an "internal colony" of American imperialism was becoming increasingly common among black militants.[9]

The argument for subsuming the entire radical movement under the ideological perspective of *anti-imperialism* reached its most sophisticated form in a pamphlet by David Gilbert of New York SDS. In "Consumption: Domestic Imperialism," Gilbert argued that:

. . . modern capitalism and its policy of imperialism has aroused political responses which have the potential to destroy it. The response to America's attempts to secure markets abroad is, increasingly, the emergence of national liberation movements. Similarly, waste production and the management of demand (domestic imperialism) seems to be leading to the development of a large-scale domestic movement (a New Left) reacting against meaningless jobs and manipulative consumption. In fact, the development of some of the industries key to the survival of modern capitalism (e.g., mass media, mass education) themselves contain the roots of its potential destruction. For people—especially the young and the blacks—are becoming more and more aware of the gap between potential social wealth and the reality of their own lives, whether in the ghetto, in the classroom, or on the job.[10]

Though Gilbert's use of a term like *imperialism* to describe the most advanced forms of contradiction in domestic capitalist development seems inverted, it is expressive of the need to show the links between the foreign and domestic aspects of capitalist development.

The honest confusion about the strategic relationship between the New Left movements of the advanced capitalist world and Third World liberation struggles was thrown into a new light by the unexpected revolutionary upheaval in France during May-June 1968. Suddenly, revolution was no longer a question of Third World Liberation and minority struggles in the United States. The concrete possibility of socialist revolution in an advanced capitalist society had been thrust onto the historical agenda. And French students had led the way. The lessons of France are still far from being absorbed by the New Left. Many eyes remain fixed on Havana, Hanoi, or Peking for inspiration and guidance. However, increasingly the realization is dawning that the events of France's near-revolution are the closest model which we are likely to have in the advanced capitalist world.

New Left International

The realization that the New Left was not an isolated phenomenon unique to the United States, but rather a specific historical movement common to all advanced capitalist societies, was forced on us by the independent but similar development of student movements from Berkeley to Berlin and from Paris to Tokyo. If you travelled to Paris or Berlin, you encountered the same bright-eyed young student activists passionately involved in the same political debates found in an SDS chapter meeting back home. The superficial coincidence of the initials of the German SDS (*Sozialistischer Deutscher Studentenbund*) and the American SDS could not mask the deeper historical identity. It is no accident that the two most highly developed neocapitalist societies in the West had produced a new student left which assumed a leading role in the anti-imperialist and domestic anti-capitalist movements. In fact, the key role of the student left went beyond West Germany and the United States. In Japan, the multi-factioned *Zengakuren* had played a crucial role ever since the anti-Eisenhower demonstrations of the 1950s. Most recently and spectacularly, French students joined the forces of this unofficial but dynamically real *new left international.* In other circumstances—but with striking resemblances—Warsaw, Prague, and even East Germany have produced their own forms of New Leftism.

Both the similarities and the national differences in these movements are instructive. It is the national differences which have produced the variations in strength and the peculiar relationship to other movements in the different countries.[11]

There are a variety of instructive categories and analytic frameworks which can be applied to an understanding of the phenomenon. Most important is the background of the development of a highly technological and bureaucratic neocapitalism.[12] In the United States and West Germany, the higher level of technological development has produced the greatest transformation of the work force with the attendant boom in the "knowledge industry" and an increasingly key role for higher education in multiversities. University students in these countries have begun to understand themselves as a new stratum of pre-workers, of apprentices being trained for the new jobs necessitated by the new technology. At the same time, the "culture of affluence"—compulsive individual consumption created to stabilize and expand the domestic market—has produced a unique set of contradictions and the resultant forms of cultural oppression and personal alienation.

In contrast, the new movement has been predictably smaller and less self-conscious in those capitalist nations which have lagged behind in their technological-economic development. France and Italy are the most notable examples of these relatively less advanced capitalist economies. In both countries the demands of the economy for large numbers of university-trained workers have been less urgent and the structures of higher education remain geared to the needs of another era when university training centered around the liberal arts and provided an education for the liberal professional bourgeoisie. It was not surprising that the French student revolt began at the newest, most modern campus—Nanterre—and spread from there to the ancient citadel of the Sorbonne in the Latin Quarter.

The backwardness of French education in particular has produced a variety of movements for reform. The most liberal elements among European neocapitalists, through the agencies of the Common Market, have proposed a set of reforms which, if adopted, would produce an educational system strangely resembling the multiversity of Berkeley's Clark Kerr and gear the training of students to the needs of advanced capitalist technology. The importance of the "knowledge industry" has become increasingly apparent, and the "knowledge factories" will have to be updated if countries like France are to compete successfully in the European market.

In addition to the differences in level of economic development, there were other factors which complicated the development of the international student scene even further. Only in West Germany did the New Left have almost unchallenged hegemony. Except for the small Moscow-oriented Communist Party, there existed no other important force of radical movement apart from the German SDS. In America, the demise of the Old Left was responsible for the relatively unhampered emergence of SDS, but, at the same time, the existence of a large underclass and the issue of racism have produced a more complex alignment of forces. In both France and Italy, the existence of large Communist parties based on the allegiance of major sectors of organized labor made it difficult for the weaker student movements in those countries to gain either autonomy or hegemony. In France, before the emergence of the March 22nd Movement at Nanterre, there were no large independent student organizations like German or American SDS.[13] Before Nanterre, French students remained stifled by the presence of the Communist Party, whereas the German and American movements gained strength and self-confidence which was directly related to their independent growth.

In both the long run and the short, the major question which was posed for the New Left was its ability to develop a political and organizational strategy which linked the student struggles to other sectors of the population. In this regard, the French students led the way by showing the possiblity of acting as a catalytic force capable of precipitating a crisis and thus mobilizing other sectors of the society for a general confrontation with the powers that be.

In France, the Communist Party did its best to ignore, or when that became impossible, to denounce the students as "anarchists" and "*provocateurs*" in an effort to keep the revolt from spreading to the factories and offices.[14] Working through the trade union bureaucracies, the role of the "official" Left was consistently reactionary. This was hardly the first time that the counterrevolutionary character of the Moscow-oriented Stalinist parties had been demonstrated. The domestic policies of the CPs had always been subordinated to the international line of Moscow. The faithful adherence of the French Communist Party to Moscow's "peaceful coexistence" line remained its first task. Even during the Algerian War, the most effective organizing of anti-imperialist programs (draft resistance and desertion and aid to the Algerian FLN) had occurred outside the Communist Party and was disavowed by the Party. At the same time, Communist leadership in the largest trade union federation (*Confederation Générale du Travail*—CGT) still has not developed demands which go beyond the usual bread-and-butter and social security programs of trade union politics. The strategies for structural reform in the labor movement and the demand for workers' control which has been percolating at the base for some time have been systematically excluded by the Communist Party, thus minimizing grass roots activity and castrating the labor movement of any revolutionary potential.[15]

The fact that French workers responded positively and enthusiastically to the initiatives of the students while the CGT leadership disavowed them (only to be forced to go along after the beginning of the general strike) tells the sad tale of Stalinist politics better than any other testimony.

Carrying the New Left's perspective to off-campus constituencies raises in particular the question of the differences between the New Left and the Old. If there is one fundamental lesson to be learned from the experience of

France, it is that the Leninist notions of a "vanguard party" which will *lead* the workers to socialism is obsolete and dead-ended. It was the direct action of the students in their own situation which sparked the revolt. By seizing control of the universities and transforming them into "popular revolutionary universities," the students provided an "exemplary action" which was then partially imitated by workers at all levels of national life. Unfortunately, once the workers had seized control of factories and offices, they failed to take that crucial step which could have turned revolt into revolution and spelled the end of French capitalism. That step—the reopening of the factories under direct workers' control and the transformation and reorganization of production for use rather than for profit—might have been taken had the labor and party bureaucrats not thrown themselves into the arms of the government and negotiated a wages settlement which undercut the force of the popular uprising. French workers have now had the time to reexamine their lot since inflation has wiped out their economic gains. The question remains: Next time will they take their own initiative and go beyond the limits prescribed by the labor bureaucrats, the party, and the entire capitalist establishment?

Through the experience of May-June 1968, French students learned the uselessness of Stalinist politics and Leninist organizational forms. Their effectiveness depended on their raising qualitatively new demands on their own terms within the institution of their own oppression. They abandoned the traditional stance of the authoritarian Left by refusing to be subordinated politically to trade union politics and they related to working people through their revolutionary example. It was perhaps the very passion and sincerity of their movement and its refusal to adopt the missionary condescension characteristic of the Leninists' attitude toward the workers which was most new and most potent. They raised demands relating to their own lives in a revolutionary and anti-authoritarian spirit, and shattered the responses of servility and orderliness which hold capitalist society together more strongly than the police power of the State.

Nothing irked the puritans of both the capitalist Establishment and the Old Left more than the anti-authoritarian disorderliness of the New Left. "Adventurism" or "utopianism" were the shibboleths hurled at us whether it be from the *Wall Street Journal* or *Pravda*. And little wonder, for the emergence of the New Left was as great a threat to the power of the monopoly-capitalist bureaucrats in New York as it would be to the state-socialist bureaucrats in Moscow.

We had begun by trying to find an answer to our own loneliness and despair through action and the building of political community. We were unwilling to adopt the stance of cynicism. We continued to insist that the revolution which we wanted to make, which we were engaged in making was about our lives and for life. We refused to defer existence and the search for new freedom and new life until some mythical future. To succumb to such mystification would have been to fall totally victim to capitalist ideology in its purest form; for capitalism *is* the ideology of deferred existence, of the ethics of accumulation for future power rather than production for present enjoyment. Nothing contradicts the capitalist ethic more thoroughly than the spirit of the New Left, a spirit embodied in the slogan "Now The Revolution!" The Community of Free Persons will not be built tomorrow if we do not begin to embody its values today.

POSSIBILITY AND THE PRESENT

The question can be put in other terms: Is the attempt to pose the political question (the question of revolution) in terms of the liberation of the individual consistent with the historical potential and the historical task which we face?

It was no accident that the books of Herbert Marcuse—especially *Eros and Civilization*[16]—were the most exciting works available to young Marxists in the early 1960s. Marcuse raised the question which was the motive force for our existence: Did the revolution which we wanted to make coincide with the historical possibility for putting an end to *all repressive civilization?* Did the political question at the very heart of advanced capitalist society put the question of man's liberation from all the economic, social, cultural, and erotic repressiveness of past social organization on the historical agenda? Did modern industrial society contain within itself the potential for a society such as Marx envisioned in which "the free development of each would be the precondition for the free development of all"—a potential which made utopianism *realistic.*

The remaining chapters of this book outline our attempt to address these questions. Basically we have asked whether the notion which young people have grasped in their lives and in their political work, of the possibility of human liberation from the forms of repressive-dominative civilization, actually corresponds to the objective historical situation in which we find ourselves. We admit the possibility of a contradiction in our position. On the one hand, we argue that the potential for post-scarcity which is inherent in the social productive forces of advanced capitalist society creates the potential material basis for non-repressive civilization through the elimination of alienated labor. On the other hand, we are struck by the argument that the objective (material) bases for freedom and socialism have existed ever since the last quarter of the nineteenth century and the completion of the capitalist infrastructure of modern industrial production—that, therefore, it has always been the *subjective* conditions for the achievement of socialism which have been lacking.

What seems new in the neocapitalist stage of industrial development is that the objective conditions for the development of a qualitatively different revolutionary response are now maturing. At this point we break with Marcuse's analysis in *One-Dimensional Man*.[17] Marcuse's understandable belief that modern industrial civilization is capable of creating one dimensional totalitarianism, which integrates the individual at the subjective level and therefore precludes the possibility of revolt, seems *in fact* to be negated by the emergence of the New Left. *In fact,* mass culture, mass media, and the consumer society—as instruments and products of advanced capitalist oppression—have produced their own negation.

Obviously, "alienation" and a "drop-out" phenomenon of even broad proportions are not in and of themselves a sufficient basis for a revolutionary political movement. Revolutionary historical change requires revolutionary self-consciousness. That consciousness can only develop if the New Left is willing and capable of coming to grips with its historical role—with its potential for initiating a new stage in human history—knowing who it is and what it can do.

The conditions which might lead to the development of such a consciousness are the subject of the following three chapters.

NOTES—CHAPTER 1

1. The story was used in a speech at the SDS Radical Education Conference at Princeton University, February, 1967.
2. See Todd Gitlin's "Theses for the Radical Movement," *Liberation*, Vol. 11, No. 3, May-June, 1967. Gitlin gives a succinct summary of the New Left attitude towards Old Left organizations.
3. *New Left Notes* was the house organ of Students for a Democratic Society published by its National Office in Chicago.
4. This paper was prepared by a team of New York SDS members, Bob Gottlieb, Gerry Tenney, and David Gilbert. A much shortened version of this paper appeared as "Toward a Theory of Social Change," *New Left Notes*, May 27, 1967.
5. A revised version of Davidson's pamphlet later appeared un- the title "The New Radicals in the Multiversity." Both were published by the National Office of SDS.
6. An excellent discussion of the European background of some of these notions is found in Dick Howard, "Gorz, Mallet, and French Theories of the New Working Class," *Radical America*, Vol. 3, No. 2, April-May, 1969.
7. Michael Spiegel, "The Growing Development of a Class Politics," Outgoing National Secretary's Address, *New Left Notes*, June 10, 1968. Spiegel's hesitant use of the category "oppression" is reflective of an (unjustified) uncertainty about using the term for phenomena other than the oppression implicit in material poverty.
8. Martin Verlet, "A Protest of the Young," *Liberation*, Vol. 11, No. 10, January 1967. The article was translated from the French by two Yale students at the request of Staughton Lynd.
9. See, for example, "Liberation Will Come From A Black Thing," speech by James Forman, reprinted by SDS, 1968.
10. David Gilbert, "Consumption: Domestic Imperialism," a pamphlet published by Movement for a Democratic Society (MDS) of New York City.
11. An excellent discussion of the role and variety of the European New Left was presented by John and Barbara Ehrenreich, "The European Student Movements, *Monthly Review*, Vol. 20, No. 4, September, 1968.

12. For a discussion of the historical significance of the term "neocapitalism," see Chapter III of this volume.

13. The French student movement was much quicker to realize the class role of students. The founding document of the French General Student Union (UNEF) referred to students as "young intellectual workers."

14. Daniel and Gabriel Cohn-Bendit, *Obsolete Communism: The Left-Wing Alternative*, trans. by Arnold Pomerans, New York, McGraw-Hill, 1968.

15. André Gorz, *Strategy for Labor, A Radical Proposal*, trans. by Martin A. Nicolaus and Victoria Ortiz, Boston, Beacon Press, 1967.

16. Herbert Marcuse, *Eros and Civilization*, New York, Vintage Books, 1962.

17. Herbert Marcuse, *One-Dimensional Man*, Boston, Beacon Press, 1964.

2

The Myth of the Middle Class

I

A primary aspect of social integration in advanced capitalist society is the attenuation of traditional forms of class conflict and the disappearance of clearly demarcated lines of conflict. In the period since the Second World War, dominant social ideology has perpetrated the notion of America as the "middle-class society," in which the vast majority of the population will eventually participate as equals. Americans are portrayed as moving inexorably toward a social homogeneity of middle-class classlessness— the "great White Marshmallow." The ideological shift away from Social Darwinism and laissez faire has included the notion that economic power no longer is the exclusive province of the owners of production, that there has occurred a "managerial revolution" and the development of a "people's capitalism." Pluralism in the social sciences has served to convey the impression of a political structure in which equal, or nearly equal groups vie for influence in a social arena free of any dominant force or forces.

The ideological myth of middle-class society has been the social cement which holds America together by offering the possibility of equal participation in the common dream and common self-image—no matter how unreal or illusory. The shattering of this myth and the exposure of the actual relationships of class and power has been one of the most important by-products of the political experiences of the new radical movements of the 1960s. What has been revealed is a society in which industrialization and particularly post-World War II technology has integrated more fully than ever before the majority of the population into the industrial wage-earning process, and in which the nature of the labor force itself is being transformed in long range terms to fit the needs of the new technology for increasing numbers of highly trained technical, scientific and professional workers. At the same time, corporate organization has not redistributed economic and political power, but has rather created giant pyramids of social organization—the corporate bureaucracies, which are models of top-down, authoritarian control and decision making.

The failure of the Old Left orthodoxy to comprehend these developments has resulted in the sectarian insistence on the vanguard role of the industrial working class without any realization of the transformations of the last generation. What we face when the ideological veil is torn away is not a homogeneous industrial proletariat growing larger and larger, but a highly stratified society in which the multiplicity of jobs and strata creates a vast array of work situations. This stratification extends to both organizations of production and institutions of socialization. And it is constantly subject to the dynamic forces of technological change. We are not faced with one homogeneous "working class," but a series of strata of workers, wage-earning or salaried, who know little of each others' lives and practically nothing of their communality of interests.

As for the much vaunted "middle class," it is safe to say that it scarcely exists outside the dream world of liberal ideology. The belief in the ideology of middle-class America has created enormous difficulties in understanding the roots of the student movement in advanced capitalist countries. Establishment psychologists have, on occasion, tried to point the finger at Dr. Spock, recommending good spankings as the answer to student rebellion. The New Left has been variously categorized as a group of young people manipulated by an alien force, products of the post-war baby boom going through their "restless" age, and a small minority of "paranoids" building a new fascist movement: all rather mystical and unconvincing arguments as explanations of a phenomenon which has been growing and spreading across the world. Old Left parties, still biding their time and hawking their literature to a smaller and smaller audience, continue to wait for the industrial armies of blue-collar workers to wake up, throw out their bad leadership, and follow the communist "good guys" to revolution (or to peaceful coexistence with the U.S.S.R. as the case might be). As the student movement became an increasingly vital force, the Old Left, blinded by its own version of the middle class myth, denounced students as *petit-bourgeois* and encouraged the New Left to calm down some of its revolutionary spirit and find jobs in the factories.

In January of 1969, *Fortune* Magazine, being notoriously astute about developments which concern the interests of the most influential members of its readership, published a series of articles which break through the existing establishment analyses of the New Left, and also challenge Old Left "Marxism." Editor Louis Banks begins with a worried editorial in which he concludes that the youth revolt is in fact ". . . an important sign of major change in national life, certain to affect the future development of the country and the world." [1] Fortune's discovery was that forty-two percent of young people between the ages of eighteen and twenty-four were not primarily concerned with the old stalwarts of middle class ideology—status, money, career—but rather with "the opportunity to change things rather than make out well within the existing system." [2] Fortune believes that the latter formulation will become increasingly prevalent among America's youth, and is, of course, concerned that business adapt to cope with the new "idealism" of its prospective employees.

For serious Marxists, the Fortune findings about the attitudes of young people should point to something the New Left has insisted all along—that the student movement has a real and legitimate base in the society, and that if Marxism is to be useful, it must serve as a tool for discovering the causes of the new revolt in advanced capitalist society, and address them in a way that offers a socialist alternative. Attempts have been made, both within the New Left and without, to "stretch the theory to fit reality," some serious and others merely opportunistic. They have ranged from attempts to apply certain Marxist categories such as "impoverization" and "proletarianization" to youth as a class-in-itself,[3] to refusing to recognize as "workers" such university-trained groups as teachers and social workers, but then changing the "line" after those groups have engaged in extended actions against the organization of their institutions.

But none of these approaches comes to terms with Marxism as something other than a biblical text to be quoted at appropriate moments in obscure ideological debates, or as an ideology-in-itself, a narrow and restrictive set of formulae which preclude looking at reality in much the same way that one-dimensional, plastic middle-classness precludes the examination of alternative human possibilities.

Marxist categories are only useful if they enable us to understand current social realities and particularly the student movement, both in terms of its own milieu—the colleges and universities—and in terms of its post-campus position in the larger society. Too often, in the floundering attempts at analysis in the past, the function of institutions like the multiversity has been ignored or misperceived, and thus both the roots of the New Left and its implications for the larger society have been misunderstood.

II

"In the late 1950s, the country became concerned about Soviet achievements in outer space, which seemed to indicate that they had a more advanced technology. Congress responded by passing the National Defense Education Act of 1958 . . ." [4]

This rather mild understatement of the impact of the launching of Sputnik I on the American educational scene describes perhaps the most dramatic event in the early educational careers of most of today's young movement activists. In 1957, students across the country were suddenly the object of attention as never before. Little Ivan was getting to be smarter than little Johnny, and it was going to take a concerted national effort to rectify the appalling situation. The Race for Space was begun; higher education, once reserved only for the rich, was now to be the aspiration of every American. The National Defense Education Act democratized the process by handing out scholarships and loans to those who didn't have the money, and at the same time encouraged the pursuit of certain fields of study, such as teaching and science—all in the "national interest." [5]

Beneath all the flurry of the space race lay profound implications. The post-World War II "third industrial revolution" was in full swing, with an increasing need for highly trained personnel to operate the complex machinery of the empire. Not only was there a need for more scientists and technicians, there was also a plethora of new jobs (such as advertising work) being created by the expansion of the domestic market, the creation of new products and needs, and the growth of service organizations required to distribute these products. In addition, there was a crying need for teachers to ensure that the rising educational requirements of the labor force were met. And finally, there was a need for an ever-increasing pacification force, to cope with the glaring contradictions between the new affluence and the old poverty, both at home and abroad. In the words of Clark Kerr:

> . . . The production, distribution and consumption of "knowledge" in all its forms is said to account for twenty-nine percent of the gross national product, according to Fritz Machlup's calculations; and "knowledge production" is growing at about twice the rate of the rest of the economy. Knowledge has certainly never in history been so central to the conduct of an entire society. What the railroads did for the second half of the last century may be done for the second half of this century by the knowledge industry; that is, to serve as the focal point for national growth . . ." [6]

And indeed, the lofty pursuit of knowledge began to resemble industry rather than the ivory tower. The multiversity became the instrument for the production of the most skilled workers, as college enrollment soared from about three million in 1960 to almost seven million in 1968.[7] As the new industrial forms of knowledge reached down into the primary and secondary schools, Kerr's "railroads" metaphor acquired a double edge. The "tracking system" is now a standard feature of most public schools, whereby students are channelled into courses of study which "suit their abilities." In plainer language, not everyone can go to college, so some students are encouraged to go, and given college preparatory courses. The rest are encouraged to study shop, home economics, business courses, etc.

The students who go to colleges and universities, so runs the myth, have an assured ticket of admission into the middle class, if only they perform reasonably well and get the proper piece of paper to prove it. The companion to the high level training they receive is the socialization process which characterizes the university environment, which prepares students for a life of status-conscious consumer orientation. But if the decline of the old stalwarts of middle-class values on campus—the fraternities and sororities—is not evidence enough to illustrate the breakdown of the socialization processes, the results of the *Fortune* survey ought to be. Fully forty-two percent of students would rather effect some meaningful change in their own lives and in the world than worry about to which social group they belong, or how much money they are going to make after college.

The roots of dissatisfaction with middle-class culture and values are to be found in more than just the factory-like education which has accompanied the need to mass-educate the country's youth to meet the new needs of American neocapitalism. The post-World War II era has seen an increasing abundance of products for individual consumption and the corresponding need to create a domestic market to absorb these products. The outcry of youth against a "materialistic" society is a direct response to this systematic organization of the domestic market, and the antisocial use of productive capacities which it implies. More and more obsolescent cars are produced, when what is needed is a clean, safe, and inexpensive mass transportation system. More ticky-tacky houses are built, more pollution created, when the resources exist to create a livable and harmonious environment for everyone.

Attempts by young people to develop an alternative culture and life style, whether in hippie culture or nonconsumer society, have generally been expropriated from them and used to sell even more products. Madison Avenue goes "psychedelic" and its products suddenly "turn you on." The revolt of young men against stereotyped "masculinity" becomes a whole new fashion era for men's clothing. Women can buy make-up that makes them look as if they don't have any on. Virtually any part of youth culture that can be sold, is sold, and the attempted alternative suffers a profitable death in the hands of those who sell it.

Besides the antisocial and wasteful uses to which the resources of the society are put at home, the war in Vietnam illustrates to a generation of young Americans the international consequences of the neocapitalist social order. Although it seems clear that the social bases for revolt were being laid through domestic developments, the war gave students a dramatically concrete experience of the political consequences of capitalist logic, and forced them to investigate the relationship between their lives at home and American imperialism abroad. The destruction of the myth of "free world" ideology has gone hand-in-hand with the crumbling concept of the middle class. Moreover, the notion of the "military-industrial complex" was broadened through student confrontation with the military and corporate ties of the universities. Students began to understand a military-industrial-academic complex which increasingly shaped the totality of their lives.

In terms of the student generations of the 1960s and their eventual integration into neocapitalist structures, the American governing class could have made no greater error than the prolongation of involvement in Vietnam. This politicized the youth of America in a direction which was to have consequences far beyond a single-issue anti-war movement, and, by eroding the major ideological mythologies upon which the post-World War II empire had been constructed, laid the basis for the emergence of a new and radically different world-view.

The Kennedy Administration had found a brilliant answer to the discontent and latent idealism of students by offering the possibility of "service" in the Peace Corps. By revealing the real character of America's international position, the war also revealed that the Peace Corps was simply the "Salvation Army of American imperialism." By demanding that young Americans die to quash the struggle of the Vietnamese for their national liberation, the government revealed that the "Free World" was quite simply that part of the world which was open to the *free* reign of American investments. Kennedy's dictum—"Ask not what your country can do for you, but what you can do for your country"—was turned around in the minds of thousands of young people who began to ask—"Just what is my country doing to my life and to the lives of millions of people in the rest of the world?"

III

Throughout the evolution of the student movement, both the Old Left orthodoxy and mainstream liberal ideology have failed to grasp the conditions which have enabled the New Left to gain hegemony over the radical movements of the '60s. The champions of middle-class values consider the rejection of those values nihilistic and destructive. The Old Left has accepted the myth of the middle class as it applies to students and encouraged them to look elsewhere for a base, give up their "privileges" and engage in missionary activity in the industrial working class. The ideological blindness of the Old Left not only traps its adherents in a dynamic of liberalism, but also apparently blinds them to reality. Marx's own definition of the term "middle class" or "petite bourgeoisie" was the "small independent producers and independent professional men," (who were a question mark in the class struggle, since they were sometimes against the bourgeoisie) whose superior economic power constantly threatened their own positions, and who sometimes identified with the bourgeoisie, when the existing order seemed to offer their only hope for stability.[8] Even if one stretches the application of the Marxist term to modern times to include persons with minor decision-making power, like managers and officials, the category "middle class" applied to only eleven percent of males between the ages of twenty-five and twenty-nine who had graduated from college in 1960.[9] The rest were workers in the classical sense —that is, people who sell their labor power in order to live and have no control whatsoever over the means of production.[10]

The increased enrollment in multiversities, and the sorts of jobs for which students are trained, reflect larger trends in the development of the labor force of the society as a whole. Throughout the development of capitalism from laissez faire to its present stage, the middle class has steadily dwindled, until now it is only about ten to twelve percent of the adult labor force.[11] Independent professionals, such as lawyers and doctors who have their own practice, have remained a relatively stable proportion of the working population, between one and two percent.[12] So not only is it wrong to assume that students are middle class, either when they are on campus or after they leave, it is also erroneous to assume that the industrial blue-collar worker is the only "proletarian" force within the country.

Before the movement can hope to reach the majority of working people in the nation with any sort of program, it must at least take the elementary step of defining the general trends within the labor force, and how those trends might be reflected in the consciousness and attitudes of the workers themselves. The dogmatic insistence of the Old Left on the central and exclusive role of the blue-collar work force in fomenting revolutionary change simply does not come to terms with modern-day American political economy and the profound effect of new forms of technology and social control upon the nature and composition of the labor force. Out of these changes grow not only differences in the specific situations of individual workers, but also larger consequences for the ability of capitalism itself to cope with new kinds of crises. We shall explore the implications of the latter questions later. But as a beginning, let us look at the occupational trends within the labor force as a whole.

Professional and Technical Workers

There has been the most rapid growth of any sector of the labor force in this category. Far from being a "middle class," nearly all workers in this category are without meaningful control over the work which they perform. They are also the most educated sector of the labor force, with an average of 16.2 years of schooling. Their numbers are expected to grow by a rate of forty percent by 1970 over the 1960 figures.[13]

Other White Collar Workers

There has been a steady increase in clerical and sales jobs, as might be expected with the rapid growth of domestic

marketing and the increasingly complex bureaucratic machinery needed to hold together the giant corporations of
neocapitalism. Interestingly, the only grouping among the
white-collar work force that has not shown significant increase since 1950 is that of management.[14] Average schooling for nonprofessional white collar workers is about 12.5
years, and their expected increase by 1970 around twenty-
five percent over 1960.[15]

Blue-Collar Workers

The classification of blue-collar workers includes those
employed in mining, manufacturing, transportation, public utilities, and construction. This portion of the employed labor force has grown by three and one-quarter
million since 1950, as compared with a fifteen million increase in employment overall.[16] The sector of the blue-
collar work force which has suffered most from the impact
of technological change is that of the unskilled worker,
whose numbers have dropped twenty percent between
1950 and 1960, and have continued a steady decline.[17]

Farmers and Farm Workers

The impact of technology and industrialization is perhaps
at its most dramatic in regard to agricultural production,
where a mere three and one-quarter million people produce the food for over 200 million. The lessons of the
agricultural sector are far more profound than its particular role in the labor force, and will be discussed in later
chapters.

IV

One can begin to see ever more clearly why the knowledge
industry is "so central to the conduct of an entire society."
Considering just the educational attainment of the labor

force, by 1964–66, fifty-four and nine-tenths percent had completed four years of high school or more; twenty-two and one-tenth percent had spent some time in college. By 1975 more than one-quarter of the labor force will have had at least some college training.[18] The new, highly skilled workers correspond to the needs of a domestic economy which has created new institutions that are profoundly different from those of a generation ago. It is no longer true that production of goods occupies the time of the largest sector of the work force. Automation and other labor-saving technology is fast making the worker on the line obsolete, as the production of services, knowledge and ideas takes over. To illustrate:

> From 1950 to 1964, the number of production workers employed in manufacturing has remained rather stable, oscillating around the figure 12.5 million. Meanwhile, the number of employees in non-agricultural establishments increased by about 13 million; that is, by as large a number of jobs as there were engaged in producing the huge manufacturing input of this country. But this rapid increase was not found in mining (employment declined) or in transportation and public utilities (employment stable) or in manufacturing production. Although the quantities of goods produced and handled greatly increased in the same period (about sixty-eight percent) the number of people occupied in handling and production did not increase; the productivity of their labor did.
>
> The 13 million new jobs were found in such fields as wholesale and retail trade (3 million), finance and insurance and real estate (1 million), miscellaneous services (3 million) and government (4 million).
>
> At the same time, the figure of the nonproductive employment of the manufacturing industries (i.e. management, office workers, researchers, etc.) rose by 1.8 million. Obviously the future of the labor force is in the nonproduction areas, in specialized and advanced services.[19]

The immense significance of the change becomes apparent when *Time* Magazine reports that seven percent of the work force now produce all the nation's food and manufactured goods.

V WORK, WASTE, AND THE USES OF THE UNIVERSITY

In *Growing Up Absurd,* Paul Goodman described the alienation and restlessness of American youth in part as a function of the fact that there were no longer any good jobs in the society. There is a growing realization of the fundamental truth of this proposition among the seven million students in American colleges and universities as well as among their graduated counterparts within the "new working class." Discontent, however, is by no means restricted to the college-channeled sector of America's youth. It is beginning to develop among the ranks of youth who have been channeled into factory jobs as well. In a speech given by James J. Matles, General Secretary-Treasurer of the United Electrical, Radio and Machine Workers of America (UE) the following observations were made:

> We have been witnessing a growing rebellion among students in the universities and colleges. They are challenging the *status quo* and the Establishment. They are doing this not because they are economically deprived or because they don't know where their next meal is coming from. Most of these young people in the leading universities and colleges come from well-to-do and middle-class families who are paying for their education.
>
> These young men and women have reached an ideological conviction that there is something basically wrong with our society and our system. As we watch TV and read the newspapers and see this revolt spreading, the question is being

asked—how about the workingclass youth in the shops? Why don't they participate with the students in this revolt?

The answer to this question is simple. The young people in the shops are involved in a revolt of their own, which is growing day by day. It is not based on ideology. It is not political in character. It expresses itself today solely in economic terms, but as it develops it is bound to have far-reaching political consequences.

The young worker doesn't give a damn for the company's shop rules and he drives the foremen crazy. He comes to work when he feels like it and quits his job at the drop of a hat without knowing where his next day's pay will come from.

Young workers are storming membership meetings and voting down a constantly growing number of settlements negotiated by their union leaders. They are the most militant fighters on the picket lines. They spark the work stoppages in the shops in protest against grievances and contract violations by management, while the union leadership wrings its hands and runs around publicly denouncing the stoppages as wildcat, unauthorized and illegal. These young workers are in revolt against the company Establishment in the shop and they are challenging the union Establishment as well.[20]

Among college students the revolt has taken the form of a refusal, the refusal to lend one's body and one's mind for wasteful, destructive, and inhuman needs. Although this began most dramatically in the draft resistance where young men refused to cooperate with the Selective Service System, it soon developed into a movement of resistance to institutions other than the draft. In particular, an upsurge of militant opposition to the military-industrial uses of the university began to crystallize in 1966 around opposition to college recruitment by Dow Chemical Company, makers of napalm, and then developed into a movement which questioned more deeply the whole relationship of the capitalist multiversity to corporate capitalist power in America. Students had begun to understand that not only were they pre-workers and that the middle class was a myth, but, additionally, that the multiversity contributed substantially to the nightmare of U.S. imperialist power abroad. Such was the substance of the Columbia University revolt of the spring of 1968 where students demanded an end to both Columbia's ties to the Institute for Defense Analysis and its expansion into the black community.

It would, however, be a mistake to assume that the student movement stops with a critique of military and real estate involvements of the multiversity. Out of its confrontation over these issues, the New Left has developed an analysis and radical critique of the multiversity which exposes its real role in the society and the integral relationship of this institution to the political and economic direction of advanced neocapitalist society. In summary, the New Left's understanding of the multiversity includes several important points:

(1) THE MULTIVERSITY: The old "liberal arts" university which once trained "professionals" and gave a facade of culture to the sons of the rich has been transformed (largely since the Second World War) into a new kind of institution—the multiversity. The primary function of the multiversity in advanced capitalist society is to train the highly skilled personnel which are necessary to the functioning of advanced industrial capitalism. Students are told that they are (or will. become) members of the middle class. This is a lie which obscures their real position in the society. In fact, students are not middle class —they are pre-workers, trainees for the new jobs created by advanced industrial technology.

(2) THE IMPERIALIST USES OF THE UNIVERSITY: The most advanced sectors of scientific and technological activity which are associated with the university have come to serve the repressive military needs of the American empire. Enormous amounts of money are channelled into projects for developing both "hardware" and "software" for putting down revolutionary movements abroad and insurgent movements at home. The hardware projects involve research in the "natural" sciences which produces weaponry for use in either the Third World or against students and poor people in the United States. Software involves programs of psychological and sociological control designed to deal in a nonmilitary fashion with the foreign and domestic wreckage of capitalism and imperialism. This latter category involves projects in the social sciences (which become increasingly the sciences of antisocial control.)

(3) THE DOMESTIC NEOCAPITALIST FUNCTIONS OF THE UNIVERSITY: Most students come to the university to get "an education" which is supposed to train them for "creative work" in the society. In reality, they find that there are no good jobs in the society—that there is no creative work. They discover that they are being trained to hold the American "business enterprise" together. They want to create the new world of advanced human potentiality: they find that they are being trained to sell more garbage to a society of people whose lives are increasingly defined in terms of their consumption of the garbage which is produced.

(4) THE VALUE-CREATING FUNCTIONS OF THE UNIVERSITY: Learning should be a collective social enterprise in which we try to understand and develop our relationship to the world around us. A free society implies a social enterprise

in which we "pull together" and teach each other the things which our individual talents dispose us to know. However, the ethic of capitalism is the ethic of competition—and the whole structure of university life fosters competitiveness rather than cooperative effort. Students are taught to compete against each other for grades, not to learn together in a collective enterprise where those students who have special talents share their insights with their fellows. In the same vein, teachers become performers who compete for the favor of students rather than other students with more experience of certain kinds.

(5) THE UNIVERSITY AS AN AGENT OF REGIMENTATION: Like all so-called "educational" institutions in capitalist society, the university functions as an agent of preserving the repressive values of our "civilization." This means that students are taught to toe the line. They are taught to substitute ego-involvement for self-realization. They are taught that women should have "dorm-hours" and remain virgins so that these same women will orient their family lives towards commodity consumption rather than toward the free expression of loving relationships. Men are taught to worship the manners and male-chauvinist morality of the football team and the suave, unfeeling sexuality of sportscar-driving *Playboy* manhood. All of the mechanisms of regimentation exist in the university so that students will fit into the slots created for them in the society, and function in the commodity relationships which capitalism creates.

The uses of the university sketched above are intimately related to the important change capitalism has undergone in the last forty years. Sometime in the decade after the First World War, American capitalism reached a stage of productivity which transformed its basic problems from the *production* of goods to the *distribution* of goods. Beginning in 1929, American capitalism experienced its most severe and most prolonged economic crisis of overproduction. This economic crisis, the result of the new level of productivity, was solved with the policies of neocapitalism. Neocapitalism simply implies the stage of development where the systematic organization and exploitation of the domestic market becomes a primary thrust of capitalist organization. It expresses itself in the promotion of compulsive individual consumption (the consumer society promoted by Madison Avenue, consumer credit and *Playboy*) and in the development of large-scale production for waste (both military production *per se* and the phenomenon of built-in obsolescence). As a result, students and their new working class counterparts are being increasingly trained for *antisocial and nonproductive work*. Teachers are not trained to teach but rather to be cops in the classroom. Engineers are not trained to build a free and human world, but to design obsolescence into cars or to perfect weaponry. Scientists are not trained to discover the nature of the universe, but to build better bombs and better bacteria for the suppression of revolutionary movements. Science and technology have been transformed into corporate "research and development" for the more effective exploitation and domination of mankind.

All of these problems arise out of the basic contradiction in capitalism: the necessity to produce more and more commodities in order to produce more and more profit for those who own and control the means of production. All of our lives and all of our relationships have been transformed into commodities and commodity relationships. Human life has become a question of producing and consuming more things rather than a question of the achievement of freedom and meaningful relationships and work.*

* Much of this analysis was presented as a programmatic proposal to the Austin, Texas chapter of SDS in September, 1968 under the title "The

VI BEYOND THE CAMPUS: STUDENTS AND CLASS

Throughout the 1960s there have been intense debates within the New Left about the question of the relation of students to other groups in the population in terms of the problem of building a majoritarian movement for radical social change. Behind the various programmatic proposals which have been advanced stand two discernible positions which can be described in terms of their understanding of the class position of students and university trainees but which also bear directly on much deeper questions of revolutionary style, strategy and goals. The two positions have been roughly divided between those who call themselves "Marxist-Leninists" on the one hand, and those who have a specifically non-Leninist approach on the other.

Briefly, the Leninist position continues to regard students as middle class, or more accurately, as members of the "petit-bourgeois intelligentsia." In this view, students conform fairly accurately to the situation in Tsarist Russia in 1902 when Lenin wrote "What is to Be Done?"; their primary task consists in bringing the message of socialist revolution to the industrial proletariat which constitutes the real force for the revolutionary transformation of society. As such, "Leninism" does not recognize an independent role for the student movement any more than it conceives of a revolutionary role for the middle class as such. In general, the "petite bourgeoisie" is regarded as a stratum whose own demands are reactionary, but which will provide certain vanguard elements (drop-outs) who can relate to the industrial proletariat through their participation in a *vanguard party*, a revolutionary elite. Students as

Uses of the University" and was reprinted by the University of Texas New Left Education Project (NLEP), a subdivision of Austin SDS.

students are not seen as a revolutionary force because they are not part of the industrial proletariat any more than this middle class as middle class is revolutionary in and of itself. Only by allying themselves with blue-collar workers in the factories can students play a revolutionary role. By no means are they to fight for their own demands as students.

The history of this controversy is complex. It was inherent in the civil rights struggle of the early 1960s, but only reached its culmination as a result of the "Black Power" position elaborated by SNCC in 1965–66 which excluded whites from the most important student-led organization in the South. Even before that, however, New Leftists in SDS had begun to turn to constituencies other than rural Southern blacks. In 1964, SDS elaborated its Economic Research and Action Project (ERAP) which turned to the poor and unemployed of the urban ghettos as a social base with a strategy for the creation of an "interracial movement of the poor." Of the ten original projects for organizing in northern ghettos, only two (a black organizing project in Newark and a poor-white organizing project in uptown Chicago) succeeded in creating successful community organizations, and none really justified the original hopes of the organizers. Furthermore, the development of a series of ghetto explosions beginning in 1964 and reaching its peak in the spring of 1968 made it clear that social rebellion among the so-called "underclass" (those forced out of production) had an energy and direction all its own.

Although ERAP did not develop a Leninist analysis of the role of students,* it continued to regard them largely

---

* ERAP was compared, with some justification, to the Russian populist (Narodnik) movement in which students and others went "to the people" (mainly the peasants).

in the role of "catalysts" for movements largely outside their own milieu, and offered no other analysis of the position of students in the universities than the liberal ideological notion of middle class.

The revival of traditional Leninist concepts within a sector of the New Left since 1966 has gone hand in hand with the elaboration of the alternative perception and analysis about pre-workers and "the new working class." Arguing that the blue-collar workers are the only authentic revolutionary force in the society, Leninists vehemently denounce the efficacy of the student movement as such, reject demands for "student power" as petit-bourgeois and reactionary, and call for a "worker-student alliance," which really implies the subordination of the student movement to a blue-collar movement which, at least for the moment, hardly exists. In addition, the Leninist position regards the libertarian, anti-authoritarian and decentralist convictions of most New Left students as symptoms of "petit-bourgeois anarchism."

The most cogent formulation of a non-Leninist approach to the question of students and other strata came out of the March 22nd Movement and the general strike in France in 1968. The notion of students speaking to other sectors of the population through "exemplary actions," through their own demands for control and transformation within their own life situation, was central to the outlook and success of the revolt. It was a clear rejection of Leninist concepts of vanguard parties and of elitist condescension. It recognized the legitimate nature of student demands and the key importance of the student movement as such. And it embodied and maintained throughout the course of the struggle its libertarian, anti-authoritarian and decentralist spirit and practice.

In his book, *Obsolete Communism: The Left-Wing Alternative,* Daniel (The Red) Cohn-Bendit cites a manifesto of one of the revolutionary student groups of the provinces, the *Enragés de Caen,* as a model of the libertarian alternative to Leninist and Stalinist attitudes and practice:

1) The students have ushered in a university revolution. By their action they have made clear to one and all how basically repressive our educational institutions really are. They began by questioning the authority of their professors and the university administration and pretty soon they found themselves face to face with the CRS. They have proved that their Rector derives his powers from the Prefect of Police. Their action at the same time revealed the unity of interest of all the exploited and oppressed classes. It is in response to the movement born at Nanterre and continued at the Sorbonne in the face of police aggression, that the workers, the ordinary soldiers, the journalists, the research workers, and the writers have joined the battle.

2) However, as soon as the workers came out on strike and the students tried to show their active solidarity with them, they came up against the CGT, which asked them not to interfere. While many students tell themselves that this is not the attitude of the majority of workers, they nevertheless feel rejected as middle class. Quite a few students who were only too anxious to follow the lead of the working class are becoming disenchanted as the workers scorn them and refuse to take them seriously. Disenchantment is particularly strong among those students who were last to join the movement, and are really more interested in achieving a few concessions than in changing society as a whole. The more progressive students, by contrast, realize that, unless the revolution finishes off capitalism and the old universities with it, there can be no real change for the better. Hence they persist, often without hope, in offering their services to the workers, beginning to feel ashamed of being students.

3) Students must rid themselves of these false feelings of guilt. Although their action sprang from the university, it has a validity that far transcends the narrow academic walls.

First of all, and most important, students must realize that the problems of the university are not irrelevant to the problems of industry. True, in industry, the workers carry the main weight of exploitation, the ownership of the means of production is in the hands of a hostile class, and the decisive struggle is played out within the productive process. But a mere change of ownership, such as the transfer of economic power from private to State enterprise, will in no way put an end to exploitation. What characterizes the structure of modern industry is not only the division between capital and labor, but also the division between supervisors and supervised, the skilled and the unskilled. The workers are exploited economically but also they are reduced to the role of mere pawns, by having no say in the running of their factories, no part in decisions that affect their own fate.

The monopoly of capital invariably goes hand in hand with a monopoly of power and knowledge.

Now, this is precisely where the students can show the way. They attack the self-styled custodians of authority and of wisdom; those who, on the pretext of dispensing knowledge, preach obedience and conformism.

Rather than waste their time analyzing the connection between the university and other social sectors, students must proclaim that the same repressive structures are weighing down on them and the workers alike, that the same mentality thwarts the creative intelligence of individuals and groups everywhere. It is in the universities that this mentality structure is elaborated and maintained, and to shake it, we must shake the entire society—even though we still do not know the quickest path to that goal.

That shaking will surely come: we can already see its signs in the protests which are rising now, not only from the working class but also from the middle class, from the press, radio and television, from artists and writers, from Catholic, Jewish and Protestant youth who have suddenly rebelled against an oppressive theology.

The struggle of the students has opened the floodgates; it

matters little that this struggle was born in a petit-bourgeois environment—its effects involve the whole of society.

Moreover, it is a far too literal and ill-digested Marxism that tries to explain everything in terms of the antagonism between the workers and the middle class. This antagonism itself springs from an economic, social and political basis. Every attack against this basis, no matter from what source, has a revolutionary bearing.

4) Students must not fear to make themselves heard and instead of searching for leaders where none can be found, boldly proclaim their principles—principles that are valid for all industrial societies and for all the oppressed of our time.

These principles are:

To take collective responsibility for one's own affairs, that is, self-government;

To destroy all hierarchies which merely serve to paralyze the initiative of groups and individuals;

To make all those in whom any authority is vested permanently responsible to the people;

To spread information and ideas throughout the movement;

To put an end to the division of labor and knowledge, which only serves to isolate people one from the others;

To open the university to all who are at present excluded;

To defend maximum political and intellectual freedom as a basic democratic right.

Cohn-Bendit goes on to comment:

In affirming these principles, the students are in no way opposing themselves to the workers. They do not pretend that theirs is a blueprint for the reconstruction of society, even less a political program, in the conventional sense of the word. They do not set themselves up as teachers. They recognize that each group had the right to lay down its own claims and its own methods of struggle. The students speak in the universal language of revolution. They do not deny that they have learned much of it from the workers; but they can also make a contribution of their own.[21]

VII LIBERTARIANISM VERSUS THE POLITICS OF GUILT

Behind the arguments and statistics about the structure of the American economy and the debates about class analysis, lies another more important dimension of the political debate now raging in the meetings of the New Left. It is a much more fundamental debate about the content of a radical political movement, its notion of human freedom, and its convictions and vision of a free society.

The libertarian position begins with the felt sense that all repressive-oppressive modes of social organization which inhibit the free development of the individual are inimical to the real interests of human beings in society. It regards the authoritarian structures of bureaucratized society as well as the taboos of repressive civilization as contrary to the health and freedom of people everywhere, and as obstacles to love, creativity and real community. It sees the close interrelationship between authoritarianism, militarism, sexual repression, and the dominative and exploitative goals and dynamics of capitalist society. It realizes that at the social-psychological level, guilt and fear divide human beings not only from each other, but also from themselves—from their loving, creative, erotic potential as persons. It rejects a political perspective which attempts to build a movement on the bases of guilt, elitism, fear, and manipulation.

Libertarian socialism—the "left-wing alternative," as Cohn-Bendit names it—rejoins a human tradition of faith in the repressed humanity of human beings with a conviction that the "kingdom" is indeed within us, that there is something "inalienable" about human life, that revolutionary politics grows out of human convictions about life itself, convictions which are there in all oppressed people, hidden behind the veil of ideology and sustained by societally induced guilt and self-hatred. It is a political and human perspective which welcomes the black man's insistence on the goodness of being black, because black identity is the path to authentic selfhood among black people, and because it challenges us in white America to reclaim our own selfhood in the midst of a life-denying civilization.

It is also a perspective which argues that we must begin now—"that if we want to create the preconditions for revolution, then we must begin to live revolutionary lives." And, it is a perspective which begins to understand that its "utopianism" and "anarchist immediatism" is both historically necessary and historically possible. That human freedom is scientific. That the Revolution is about our lives.

NOTES—CHAPTER 2

1. "The Editor's Desk," *Fortune* Magazine, Vol. LXXIX, No. 1, January, 1969, page 57.
2. "What they Believe," *ibid.*, p. 70. *Fortune's* explanation of how the survey was conducted: "In the . . . survey, taken last October, 718 young men and women aged eighteen through twenty-four, were interviewed . . . The group was representative as to race, sex, marital status, family income, and geographic region. Those who were attending college at the time of the survey (334) were deliberately over-sampled, in order to make possible a more detailed presentation of their views. However, in the comparisons tabulated . . . the college and non-college groups have been reweighted so as to adjust for this oversampling."
3. For a careful and serious examination of the youth-as-class concept, see John and Margaret Rowntree's article "Youth as a Class in the *International Socialist Journal,* February, 1968.

4. Jerry M. Rosenberg, *Automation, Manpower, and Education,* New York, Random House, 1966, p. 107.

5. *Ibid.*

6. Clark Kerr, "The Frantic Race to Remain Contemporary," in Robert S. Morison, ed., *The Contemporary University,* Boston, Houghton, Mifflin Co., 1966, p. 27.

7. U.S. Bureau of the Census, *Statistical Abstract of the United States: 1968,* No. 187, (89th Edition), Washington, D.C., 1968, p. 128.

8. T. B. Bottomore, *Classes in Modern Society,* New York, Pantheon Books, 1966, and Marx and Engels, *The Communist Manifesto.*

9. *Fortune, op. cit.,* p. 73.

10. Of these, about two-thirds were in the "professional and technical" fields.

11. Leonard Reissman, *Class in American Society,* Glencoe, Ill. Free Press, p. 307, and *Statistical Abstract, op. cit.,* p. 226.

12. *Ibid.*

13. Sam Bass Warner, ed., *Planning for a Nation of Cities,* Cambridge, MIT Press, 1966.

14. *Statistical Abstract, op. cit.,* p. 226.

15. *Statistical Abstract, op. cit.,* p. 225.

16. *Statistical Abstract, op. cit.,* p. 223.

17. *Statistical Abstract,* No. 310, p. 215.

18. Dennis F. Johnston, "Education of Adult Workers in 1975," *Monthly Labor Review,* Vol. 91, No. 4, Washington, Bureau of Labor Statistics, Department of Labor, April, 1969, p. 10ff.

19. William A. Williams, *The Great Evasion,* Chicago, Quadrangle Books, 1964, p. 85.

20. Reprinted in pamphlet form as "The Young Worker Challenges The Union Establishment," New York, UE Publication 485–J–12–68.

21. Cohn-Bendit, *op. cit.,* pp. 88–90.

3

Neocapitalism and the New Contradictions

The appearance of the New Left in the advanced capitalist countries is the direct result of the development of new objective conditions and new economic, social, and political contradictions. Its political activists are people (especially young people) who are expressing human needs which break radically with the dominant culture and point toward a qualitatively different life and civilization. This development has far-reaching implications for the future of the left in the industrialized world and for world revolutionary development. The failure to understand these new historical developments and their implications has led to considerable confusion both within and without the movement. The failure of the old Marxist-Leninist orthodoxy to face this new reality is basic to the dogmatic misunderstanding which characterizes the attitude of the Old Left towards new leftists.

Most importantly, it seems clear that material scarcity did not provide the basic conditions for the development of the New Left's negation of capitalist society in the industrialized world. The New Left is a reaction to societies characterized by a high level of individual consumption for an important segment of the population, production for waste in previously unimaginable proportions, and the relegation of the "class struggle" in the form of the fight for higher wages to the arena of collective bargaining for an increasingly large slice of an increasingly large pie. This is not to deny that poverty is the determining fact of life for an important segment of the population. The rural and urban poor and unemployed account for perhaps as much as twenty percent of the population of the advanced industrial world, and poverty remains the fundamental economic condition of much of the neocolonial Third World. Nevertheless, it is in the midst of the consuming strata of the consumer society that the New Left has grown and rebelled. Furthermore, poverty in the advanced capitalist world will not provide the basis for a broadly based movement for radical social transformation.[1]

The Third Stage of Capitalism

The last generation has witnessed the internal transformation of capitalist society in dimensions which are sufficient to assume the form of a new stage of capitalist development. The nature of this new era determines the conditions for the revolt of the New Left. We can best describe this development in terms of the following historical framework of three stages of capitalist development:[2]

(1) LAISSEZ FAIRE: Capitalism established itself, in different countries at different times, by overthrowing the feudal and mercantilist systems which it had subverted internally over a long period of time. The basic achievement of all these crucial revolutions (particularly the English, American, and French) was to allow the new capitalist classes to replace the old feudal and aristocratic structures with a new social and political order which would permit the reorganization of production for the greater extension of the capitalists' power—that is, the power to accumulate more and more surplus value. The ideology of laissez faire was basically a justification for letting the capitalists "do their thing," uninhibited by state control or any larger human or social considerations. The ideology of laissez faire argued that by allowing the free play of capitalist dynamics, society would automatically create the best of all possible worlds.

(2) MONOPOLY CAPITALISM: The internal dynamics of capitalism, the tendency for the mechanism of competition to eliminate competition by weeding out the less competitive, destroyed laissez faire from within. This tendency toward monopoly was (despite the Ayn Rand romanticists) an inevitable result of capitalism itself. A secondary manifestation of the concentration of capital as Monopoly Capital was the development of modern economic imperialism. The search for markets and raw materials was as old as the expansion of Western civilization beyond its European borders. But, as more and more economic power was concentrated in the hands of fewer and fewer financiers (the "finance capital" of Hilferding) a new factor, the desperate search for *outlets for investment* became the central focus of capital's foreign policy. The period from about 1870 to the First World War was characterized by the "carving up" of the rest of human society into "empires" and "spheres of market influence."

The scramble for world empire eventually produced conflicts between the capitalist nations which were the basis for the first major struggle for capitalist hegemony—the First World War. After that war had already begun

Lenin wrote his pamphlet, "Imperialism: The Highest Stage of Capitalism," which explained what was happening in terms of an analysis of this second (Monopoly) stage of capitalism. That pamphlet became a canonical work for the Communist Movement (Third International) which developed as a sequel to the triumph of the Bolsheviks in Russia. In retrospect, one might argue that Lenin's pamphlet should have been called, "Imperialism: The Most Dramatic External Manifestation of the Stage of Monopoly Capitalism." But Lenin's world-historical perspective turned the eyes of the next generation of the Left away from the internal structures and struggles of advanced capitalist society toward the nonindustrialized Third World and its struggles of national liberation. This strain of theory reaches its culmination in the perspective of Mao Tse-tung and Lin Piao, who see the central conflict of our time as the struggle between the "peasant villages" of the Third World and the "capitalist cities" (including those of the Soviet Union) of the industrialized "metropolis."

In addition, the Leninist formulation includes an explanation for the present nonrevolutionary ("opportunist") character of the industrial working class in the capitalist world. Lenin had argued that the "super profits" of imperialism have enabled the governing classes to "buy off" a privileged stratum of workers (the "labor aristocracy") who were responsible for the conservative political direction of the trade unions.[3]

(3) NEOCAPITALISM: THE THIRD STAGE OF CAPITALIST DEVELOPMENT: The historical perspective presented by Lenin is inadequate to describe the evolution of advanced capitalist society. The New Left has finally had to come to terms with the internal history of capitalist society itself.

We are living in the third stage of capitalist development, a stage which is called variously "neocapitalism" or "corporate capitalism." After the stages of laissez faire and of monopolization, capitalism has entered a new era of development. Just as the era of laissez faire was characterized by competition and the building of the infrastructure of capitalist industrialization, and the era of monopoly capitalism was characterized by the consolidation of control by finance capital and the conquest of foreign markets through imperialism, so the third stage of development, neocapitalism, is characterized by the control of the economy by the giant corporations and the intensive expansion and development of investment, production, and the market within the advanced capitalist nations. The result is that a large majority of the "super profits" of capitalism are being reaped from domestic capitalist investments rather than from investment abroad.[4]

This New Left formulation runs counter to the classical position of the Old Left as derived from Lenin's work itself. Lenin did not foresee this development of neocapitalism. In fact, he argued that it was impossible. He stated:

It goes without saying that if capitalism could develop agriculture, which today lags far behind industry everywhere, if it could raise the standard of living of the masses, who are everywhere still poverty stricken and underfed, in spite of the amazing advance in technological knowledge, there could be no talk of a superabundance of capital. This "argument" the petit-bourgeois critics of capitalism advance on every occasion. But if capitalism did these things it would not be capitalism; for uneven development and wretched conditions of the masses are fundamental and inevitable conditions and premises of this mode of production. As long as capitalism remains what it is, surplus capital will never be utilized for the purpose of raising the standard of living of the masses in a given country, for this would mean a decline in profits for the capitalists, but for the purpose of increasing profits by exporting capital abroad to the backward countries.[5]

This analysis, advanced by Lenin in 1917, reveals precisely the inadequacy of his outlook and points the way toward an alternative understanding of the nature of our own era, the neocapitalist era, which began to take shape in the period following World War I. In this new stage, capitalism has done precisely those things which Lenin argued it could not do—it has developed agriculture through the application of industrial technology (mechanization and agricultural science); it has raised the living standards of the masses within the capitalist countries (through the development of the internal consumer market); and it has even created additional, nonproductive outlets for investment in the development of waste production (military investment and a variety of planned obsolescences).

Although these developments are contrary to Lenin's analysis and to the vulgar economic determinism of the Old Orthodoxy (inevitable impoverization of the masses), they lead toward (rather than away from) an understanding of the real possibility and necessity of a revolutionary socialist transformation of capitalist society. What is required, however, is a much deeper understanding of the meaning of socialism and its potential for human liberation *and* a new strategy and new approach embodying an understanding of the new contradictions in neocapitalism, plus the conscious redefinition of the meaning of those values which are inseparable from a truly socialist perspective—freedom, democracy, and human creativity. It is precisely in these directions that the New Left must move if it is to develop a *radical* challenge to capitalism.

It is no longer sufficient that one-fifth of the population in neocapitalist societies lives in conditions of material scarcity. These strata of the people are either outside the labor force as urban unemployed or are represented by dispersed rural populations forced out by agricultural industrialization. The human misery of these groups is testimony not only to the inhumanity and social irrationality of capitalist society but also to the fact that advanced technology is making work less necessary. The plight of displaced rural populations in the urban ghettos is made all the more hopeless by the fact that those jobs which are being created in the economy require highly skilled or highly educated labor. Millions of European peasants came to America at a time when industrialization required masses of unskilled laborers. Poor blacks and poor whites have been forced off the land in the last generation at a time when blue-collar jobs were diminishing and new job opportunities were opening up in the technical, professional, and scientific areas. The sons and daughters of white workers may receive the schooling which enables them to move into skilled, technical or professional jobs while the sons and daughters of Southern poor black and poor white farmers or Mexican-American farm laborers move into the poverty and unemployment of the urban ghettos and barrios. Although these are the most materially oppressed sectors of the population, neither the unemployed of the cities nor the rural poor are an adequate social base for a revolutionary socialist movement because of their peripheral relationship to the means of production. Material scarcity continues to be an agonizing problem among a minority of the population, but it is no longer the only issue around which a majoritarian movement, which would raise demands capable of radically challenging the capitalist system, can be built.

Furthermore, the Leninist analysis of the situation of the industrial workers begs the real question. The problem is much more profound than the analysis of super profits and the buying off of a labor aristocracy. A much more basic phenomenon involves the *integration* of trade union demands for higher wages and shorter hours. After the period of primitive capital accumulation and the building of the economic infrastructure of industrial production, the need for the maintenance of wages and hours at their Draconian, mid-nineteenth century levels was less and less pressing. It became possible for capitalists to raise both real wages *and* real profits with rising per capita productivity. In fact, with the introduction of the new production techniques of the 1920s (and finally the methods of automated and cybernated production of the '50s and '60s), rising consumption levels among all working strata of the population became necessary to the economic survival of capitalist production—necessary in order to absorb the increased product and to avoid the cyclical crises of overproduction.

Thus the determinist theses of the Old Left—increasing material impoverishment and inevitable economic breakdown—are rendered less central by the internal development of advanced capitalism. Increased consumption to provide a growing domestic market and government intervention in order to stabilize the business cycle have become major concerns of the "enlightened" wing of the corporate governing class. This drawing together of corporate economic power and the structures of the state apparatus has yielded a variety of bureaucratic state capitalism which brings all aspects of social and economic existence under greater and greater centralized control. This development has been necessitated by a problem peculiar to advanced capitalism: the proportion of constant capital (plant and equipment) to variable capital (wages) has been inverted. It is no longer necessary to support lay-offs and decreased production because the proportion of investment devoted to machinery is so much greater than that devoted to wages that investment cannot be amortized unless full production (and fuller consumption) is maintained.[6]

The New Contradictions

Due to the new needs of the productive apparatus, one of the chief characteristics of neocapitalism involves the intensive organization of the domestic capitalist market under the leadership of the giant corporations. This development is closely linked to the rising level of per capita productivity in the decade following World War I when per capita productivity rose at an unprecedented rate— largely as a result of the new assembly-line technology of the so-called "second industrial revolution." This rising productivity plus the relative rigidity of wage levels due to the weakness of the labor movement led eventually to capitalism's most profound and extended "crisis of overproduction."

The Great Depression did not correct itself as prior business fluctuations had done. Falling wages and prices and surging unemployment did not produce a new market equilibrium which would restimulate production and investment. Instead it was necessary to abandon the old laissez faire viewpoint (government hands off the economy) in favor of a variety of state controls and interventions designed to guarantee investment opportunities, maintain steady expansion of the consumer market, and thus stabilize the business cycle. These measures, first adopted as emergency measures by New Deal type governments in the 1930s became permanent features of most western capitalist economies after the Second World War. Deficit financing and pump-priming, government support of income levels (including government-supported collective bargaining), subsidies for giant corporations and noncompetitive State consumption for waste (military budgets)—all of these familiar neocapitalist measures are essential to the survival of advanced capitalism. In addition, there are other features of neocapitalist society which determine and transform the nature of social and cultural oppression. Consumer financing, advertising, and the media all contribute to the increasing promotion of individual consumption of commodities as the way of life and the definition of existence under neocapitalism.

The possibility for a society of "post-scarcity" and fully automated production becomes the historic potential of our era. This in itself is producing a new kind of crisis in capitalism and a new kind of political awareness among socialists in the New Left. It is our task to organize in such a way that people begin to grasp the meaning of this historic human potential and to understand the way in which its realization is frustrated under capitalism. It is important that we present an understanding of what socialism could mean in the society with the greatest revolutionary potential in the history of mankind.

Marx seems to have perceived the possibility that it might be in conditions like those which are developing in advanced neocapitalism that the potential for a socialist revolution would also develop. He wrote:

> To the degree that large-scale industry develops, the creation of real wealth comes to depend less on labor-time and on the quantity of labor expended, and more on the power of the instruments which are set in motion during labor-time, and whose powerful effectiveness itself is not related to the labor-time immediately expended in their production, but

depends rather on the general state of science and the progress of technology. . . . Large industry reveals that real
wealth manifests itself rather in the monstrous disproportion
between expended labor-time and its product, as well as in
the qualitative disproportion between labor, reduced to a
pure abstraction, and the power of the productive process
which it supervises. Labor no longer appears as an integral
element of the productive process; rather man acts as super-
visor and regulator of the productive process itself. . . . He
stands at the side of the productive process, instead of being
its chief actor. With this transformation, the cornerstone of
production and wealth is neither the labor which man directly expends, nor the time he spends at work, but rather
the appropriation of his own collective productive power, his
understanding of nature and his mastery over nature, exercised by him as a social body—in short, it is the development
of the social individual. The theft of other peoples' labor-
time on which contemporary wealth rests, appears as a mis-
erable basis compared to this new one created by large-scale
industry itself. As soon as labor in its direct form has ceased
to be the great wellspring of wealth, labor-time ceases and
must cease to be its measure, and therefore exchange-value
the measure of use-value. . . . With that, the system of production based on exchange-value collapses. . . . Capital is
its own contradiction-in-process, for its urge is to reduce labor-time to a minimum, while at the same time it maintains
that labor-time is the only measure and source of wealth.
Thus it reduces labor-time in its necessary form in order to
augment it in its superfluous form; thus superfluous labor
increasingly becomes a precondition—a question of life or
death—for necessary labor. So on the one side it animates
all the powers of science and nature, of social coordination
and intercourse, in order to make the creation of wealth
(relatively) independent of the labor-time expended on it.
On the other side it wants to use labor-time as a measure for
the gigantic social powers created in this way, and to re-
strain them within the limits necessary to maintain already-

created values as values. Productive forces and social relations—both of which are different sides of the development
of the social individual—appear to capital only as means,
and material conditions to blow this basis sky-high.[7]

Whether Marx in fact ever perceived the possibility of
economic conditions like those we face a century after his
writing should not be the major concern of the New Left.
Rather than rescuing Marx from the Marxists, we should
be concerned with saving our movement from destruction
and making it relevant to our people. Understanding the
nature of the socio-economic conditions which confront us
is one way of clarifying our own perceptions.

Compulsive Consumption and Waste

When Establishment sources express the fear that a new
generation of young Americans is rejecting consumption
as a goal and definition of their lives, it expresses a very
real concern on the part of the corporate establishment
about its economic future and its historical *raison d'etre*.
In place of isolation, powerlessness, meaningless work,
and lives defined as the production, ownership, and consumption of commodities, they are demanding community, love, creativity, and power over their own lives. It is
a revolt of being, of Eros, against the plastic, boring, dehu-
manizing world, with its values of domination and exploitation, which brutalizes two-thirds of the world's people in
order to maintain power and profit abroad while creating
an anesthetized and de-eroticized plastic population in the
midst of a garbage heap at home.

Neocapitalist society, with its emphasis on compulsive
individual consumption, waste production, and mass culture, lays the basis for the "one-dimensional society"[8]
which Marcuse describes so eloquently. The need for the
total organization of economic life leads also to the totalitarian organization of culture and ideology. At the level of

cultural life, mass culture becomes both a product for sale and a mechanism of social control and pacification. Mass media not only fill the compulsive neurotic needs which maintain the domestic market, but also produce the canned news which maintains the dominant ideology. Because neocapitalism demands steadily increasing consumption, it requires a break with the ideologies of scarcity which previously justified class society and provided solace for a suffering humanity.

In its ideological development, the governing class can no longer rely on the Church and its puritan version of Christian religion. Both *simplicity* and *otherworldliness* conflict with the economic needs of the day. Jesus of Nazareth must be replaced by Santa Claus (the patron saint of consumption) in the new hagiology, while *Playboy* nightclubs become the sanctuaries of the new cult of consumption and repressive desublimation. God did not die a natural death—he was simply discarded by the establishment when he no longer served their purposes. A nightclub in Philadelphia is named "The Eleventh Commandment" and advertises on its marquee: *Thou Shalt Be Entertained!*

The development of Madison Avenue techniques for the stimulation of compulsive individual consumption together with the vast expansion of consumer credit facilities has created new artificial needs for a people whose choices are limited and directed in the absence of rational economic organization for real human need and social development. Instead of a transportation system which would get people safely, quickly, comfortably, and cheaply from one place to another we are provided with a concrete-and-asphalt landscape, cars which are designed to fall apart, and slick advertising which offers us sexual fantasies in place of sexual freedom and real Eros.

When Nikita Khrushchev—the advocate in another setting of pacification through individual consumption—announced that the Soviet Union would "bury" us by out-producing American capitalism, he failed to realize that our own capitalists are already in the process of burying us in the garbage of their own antisocial productivity.

Neocapitalism and Social Pacification

The success of the neocapitalist social order depends on its ability to deliver the goods (the consumer goods) and on the willingness of the vast majority of the working population to accept individual consumption as the sole measure of its freedom and well-being. Neocapitalist reforms have never been a totally coherent program in the United States quite simply because not all American capitalists have been as enlightened about their long-range self-interest as men like FDR and RFK. Roosevelt's neocapitalist New Deal was obtained in the face of virulent opposition from those representatives of the governing class who refused to recognize that in the era of advanced capitalism the policies of laissez faire cannot cope with the real problems. Roosevelt himself never really seemed to understand the full implications of what John Maynard Keynes was proposing. And Keynes never seemed to appreciate the irrationality of what he proposed. As two contemporaries of the New Deal saw it:

> There is nothing the New Deal has so far done that could not have been done better by an earthquake. A first-rate earthquake, from coast to coast, could have reestablished scarcity much more effectively, and put all the survivors to work for the greater glory of Big Business—with far more speed and far less noise than the New Deal.[9]

Perhaps the most coherent program for neocapitalist reforms is that undertaken by the French after World War

II. Capitalist state economic planning in France has never succeeded in fulfilling the highest hopes of its architects, but that is at least partially due to the fact that one of France's most sophisticated neocapitalists, Charles De Gaulle, was excluded from power for eleven years. De Gaulle realized as early as 1946 that state planning and a close working arrangement between capital and labor could lay the basis for a new era of capitalist peace and profit. What he did not count on, apparently, was the fact that even neocapitalist society has irreconcilable contradictions. It remained for the students of Nanterre and Paris to remind him of that fact by occupying the knowledge factories. It then developed that the leadership of the CGT, having negotiated higher wages like good neocapitalist trade union bureaucrats, were disavowed by the workers who supported the students and demanded workers' control in the factories. Finally, teachers in the public schools joined the students' revolt and closed down the high schools with demands for an overhaul of the entire educational system. Even technical and professional strata such as communications staff in the national television and radio turned down the wage increase which the government offered and walked off their jobs demanding a "charter guaranteeing that the government would not pressure them to slant the news." [10]

The failure of integration and social pacification to maintain a totally docile population can only increase as the irrationality of advanced capitalist production becomes more apparent. In particular the emergence of the new technology of automation and cybernation and the potential for post-scarcity inherent in the present period creates a new vision, and the possibility of a qualitatively different kind of civilization—the possibility of nonrepressive society and the elimination of alienated labor. Such a possibility will not, however, become a political program unless the New Left is willing to organize in terms of it. Any retreat in the direction of the empty slogans of the old orthodoxy is not only a denial of reality but a denial of ourselves. As long as we fear being called "utopian" we will never be realistic, and will certainly not speak to the needs and hopes of those outside our ranks. Alongside the French students who occupied the Sorbonne in the spring of 1968 we should insist—*all power to the imagination!*

The obvious conclusion which any sensitive observer of the early industrial revolution could have reached is that a new era in human productivity was opening up which offered the revolutionary possibility for overcoming the problem of material scarcity and relegating the "struggle for survival" to the historical dust bin. The failure of industrialization to fulfill this promise is central to the development of radical social theory (utopian, socialist, and anarchist). The attempt of critical theory to develop an understanding of the inability of capitalism to realize the liberating potential of the new productive forces found its most elaborated expression in the work of Marx. There was obviously something fundamentally wrong with the capitalist system. Capitalism could be attacked from the moral and humanist viewpoint as alienating and exploitative. Marx was finally drawn to analyze it in terms of its political economy. However inadequate *Capital* may be, it remains the most comprehensive attempt to understand capitalism as an economic system and to decipher the contradictory nature of its internal dynamics.

Much of the New Left has remained justifiably uncomfortable with "Marxism" as a framework for revolutionary thought. Certainly the official mysticism of "the science of Marxism-Leninism" or "dialectical-materialism" can be rejected. Most of the recent attempts of the New Left to

integrate Marxian theory into political practice have emphasized the "early (humanist) Marx" of the 1840s or
have concentrated their efforts on the writings which directly preceded *Capital* (the *Grundrisse* and the *Contribution to the Critique of Political Economy*). This latter
emphasis returns to the intriguing historical question of
the nineteenth century: Is there a fundamental contradiction in capitalism which is based in the economic dynamics of the system itself? The answer seems to be yes, but a
very different yes than that which has been passed off as
"Marxist" and "scientific."

NOTES—CHAPTER 3

1. Andre Gorz, *Strategy for Labor, A Radical Proposal,* trans. by
    Martin A. Nicolaus and Victoria Ortiz, Beacon Press, 1967.
2. This analysis was first presented by the authors in the present
    form in a paper, "The Third Stage of Capitalism," printed as
    "Neocapitalism and the New Left" by the New Left Educa-
    tion Project, Austin, Texas, 1968.
3. V. I. Lenin, "Imperialism, The Highest Stage of Capitalism,"
    Chapter IV.
4. Ernest Mandel, "Workers Under Neo-Capitalism," *Interna-
    tional Socialist Review,* Vol. 29, No. 6, November–December,
    1968. A paper delivered at the 1968 Socialist Scholars Con-
    ference.
5. V. I. Lenin, *op. cit.*
6. David Gilbert, "Consumption: Domestic Imperialism," New
    York, Movement for a Democratic Society, 1968.
7. Karl Marx, *Grundrisse der Kritik der Politischen Okonomie,*
    quoted in Martin Nicolaus, "The Unknown Marx," *New
    Left Review,* No. 48, March–April, 1968.
8. Herbert Marcuse, *One-Dimensional Man,* Boston, Beacon
    Press, 1964.
9. Benjamin Stolberg and W. J. Vinton, *The Economic Conse-
    quences of the New Deal,* New York, Harcourt, Brace, and
    World, 1935.
10. *Wall Street Journal,* June 5, 1968, p. 1.

4

Scarcity, Post-Scarcity, and the Fundamental Contradiction

Capitalist industrialization, especially in the age of emerging cybernated production, offers the possibility for producing in abundance those material goods necessary for human survival, reproduction, and well-being, but frustrates the realization of this potential because of the necessity of maintaining the mechanisms for the appropriation of profit (surplus value). Put simply, this means that our productive resources are such that people could live without working but that capitalism requires that people work in order to live. The common-sense question might be: why not just give things away? The answer is that giving things away provides no mechanism (market) for appropriating profit, therefore people must work and earn incomes so that they can buy on the market the goods which are produced.

In its simplest terms, the fundamental socio-economic contradiction in capitalism grows out of the "work-income" relation as mediated by the market—the market for labor as well as goods. In neocapitalist society you have to work in order to live despite the fact that living without

working is the potential of capitalist economic and technological development. Instead of abolishing the market and
fully automating production in order to eliminate scarcity
and alienated work, capitalism produces more waste, more
alienating jobs, and encourages antisocial and repressive
patterns of consumption. For capitalism there is no way
out of this dilemma: the market must be maintained and
jobs must be created (however useless) and consumption
must continue to rise (even if it requires built-in obsolescence) in order that profits continue to be made no matter
what the human cost of the whole enterprise. For, human
costs are not entered in the account books of large corporations, and capitalism is a system of production for profit
rather than for use.

The first attempt to describe the implications of this
contradiction in terms of political program (at least, to the
knowledge of these authors) was embodied in a Program
Proposal at the 1968 National Convention of SDS (June
10–15, 1968, East Lansing, Michigan):[1]

> America is faced with a set of contradictions around the
> work-income connections. As Marcuse points out, technology
> has replaced labor as the central factor in productivity:
> ". . . now automation seems to alter qualitatively the rela-
> tion between dead (machines and technical knowledge) and
> living labor (workers); it tends toward the point where
> productivity is determined by the machines, not by the in-
> dividual output."
>
> This perception has broad implications for our work that
> will be considered further in the two models for the cities
> outlined below. To list them in short form: 1) Since produc-
> tivity is not related to the specific worker, it is impossible to
> define income in any traditional way. Productivity has be-
> come collective; income must also be collective. 2) Since
> earlier radical analysis has depended on the role of labor in
> the productive process as the prime contradiction, the switch

to technology drastically alters the way in which labor can be treated in future organizing efforts. 3) Since labor has had its class significance altered, it can be integrated into essential aspects of the bourgeois social structure of America. 4) This social structure is most accurately characterized by the incessant demands of consumption, demands that arise out of the needs of capitalism for continued expansion and social control. 5) The need to maintain the contradictory work-income relation and the growing pressure for social stability requires the creation of institutionalized waste and make-work. As the need for production workers decreases, more and more people are channelled into meaningless, socially worthless jobs: advertising, sales, welfare work, and other service functions.

A radical analysis starts from the belief that the total productivity of a country like America is the result of technological advances that must be seen as the property of the whole society and which must be used to meet the needs of all.

Concrete examples of this irrationality in advanced capitalism are abundantly available from the social reality which we face every day of our lives. Driving around Chicago one sees an increasing number of service stations with signs which advertise: *"One dozen eggs free with every ten-gallon purchase of gasoline."* At the same time, the Chicago police force is everywhere more apparent and increasingly aggressive. Why?—because of the danger of riots and "crime in the streets." Consider for a moment the nature of the contradiction involved in these two intimately related phenomena. On the one hand, it is apparent that the American economy is capable of producing so many eggs or so much gasoline that it is necessary to give one away in order to get people to pay for the other. Should the trend continue, we can easily imagine a time when gas stations will offer a free ham-and-eggs breakfast with every tankful of gas. Or, when restaurants will offer a free tankful of gas with every meal you purchase. Since many gas stations already offer free dinnerware with gasoline purchases (or at least trading stamps convertible into dinnerware), we could even project service stations which will offer a complete breakfast cook-out everytime you roll up to their pumps: gasoline, eggs, bacon, frying pan, charcoal briquets, and a picnic area to encourage your consumption of petroleum products.

On the other hand, black people in Chicago's West Side and South Side ghettos have looted stores occasionally in recent years. These loot-ins have led to the beefing up of the Chicago police force which, like all police forces in capitalist society, exists above all to protect private property (and the orderly exchange of human labor and goods) within a market system in which all participate and from which a few profit. The situation seems slightly absurd on its face when, while people get shot or arrested for "stealing" eggs on West Madison Avenue, other people get eggs free in the service station fifteen blocks away on North Ogden Avenue. In addition, the "solution" to the problem seems both contradictory and ineffective. The Chicago police force costs a lot of money and the prevention of "theft" (individual or collective) sometimes costs the lives of both policemen and ordinary citizens. Why not, as a cheaper and more humane solution to the problem, just set up free food stations on the West and South Sides which would be like the gas-and-eggs stations except that nobody would buy any gas?

The answer to our simple-minded proposition is, of course, direct and to the point. The people who buy gas on North Ogden have money to make their purchases which entitle them to the free eggs. The people who riot on the West Side have no money to buy anything and should therefore be shot for trying to make eggs free.

The reasoning is obviously serious. But we might push things a bit further by asking a couple more questions. First: Why don't the people on the West Side have any money? The answer (obviously): because they don't have any jobs. But why don't they have any jobs? Because (obviously) there aren't enough jobs available. But why are there not enough jobs available? Because (and we are likely to get several answers) the productivity of the economy has reached a point where it creates "surplus" labor; or, because it's more profitable to build petroleum refineries in Venezuela than to build factories in the ghettos of America; or because these people aren't trained to do the highly skilled work which the economy requires. But, we press the question a step further, why aren't the people trained for the highly skilled jobs which the economy requires?—because they came late to the urban industrial North and other groups of people were better suited to receive the advanced training for the highly skilled jobs.

Slightly confused in our naïveté at this point, we attempt to rephrase the question. Let's assume, we suggest, that the economy is already producing so much excess foodstuffs and dishes (as the behavior of the petroleum companies would suggest) and that (as has been suggested) large numbers of people are no longer needed for the productive process at all. Why then couldn't we just let the people who aren't needed as workers consume the growing excess production?

Slightly baffled by our obvious lack of sophistication, the man-on-the-spot calls in several expert witnesses. The first, a sociologist with a Ford Foundation grant, informs us that: "People who don't work are socially unstable. The large number of unemployed in the ghettos has been the most direct cause of the riots." The second, a government-

employed psychologist says: "People who do not undergo
the basic socialization process of living by working and
living to work fail to integrate into the dominant social
patterns of production and consumption. They suffer an
attendant identity crisis and tend to express their ag-
gressiveness by striking out against the symbols of the
dominant culture. Or, they tend to create a subculture
of alternative values which deny, but are fundamentally
conditioned by, the dominant system. In brief, they either
become rioters or the contemporary equivalent of the
zootsuited street hustler." The third, a professional economist temporarily in the hire of the Urban Coalition of liberal capitalist elements, has this to add: "The ghetto resi-
dent came into the economy at a time when the traditional
avenues for upward-boundness were largely closed. He
had no way of either assimilating into the capitalist system
by creating his own petite bourgeoisie or of moving into
the traditional industrial sectors of the economy. He finds
himself, therefore, alienated from the traditional channels
of economic advancement. Our job is to make available
capital resources which would otherwise be more profitably employed in investments abroad to a certain sector of
the ghettoized population so that this sector can create a
capitalist image of its future. We understand that this may
involve certain financial sacrifices on the part of the established resources of the country; but those sacrifices are ab-
solutely necessary to the maintenance of the health of the
economic and social system under which we live." The
fourth, a Kennedy administration left-over from the Job
Corps, gives another opinion: "Technological advancement has created a hard-core of unemployables who cannot
be absorbed into the traditional economic roles assigned
to lower-income and immigrant groups in the population. Because of the instability of this stratum, we find

it necessary to retrain them for new roles in the future of the country. Although many young men from the ghetto have been turned over to us beyond the age where they could be trained for advanced industrial positions, we find that a few weeks or months of rigorous training suits them admirably for service in the armed forces of our great nation; besides, they will make excellent policemen in their home towns when they return."

All these admirable attempts to deal in a most complicated fashion with a problem which had once seemed to us quite simple (the problem of the eggs, the gasoline, and the riots) leave us wondering whether common sense should be abandoned or if there might not be a much simpler and more rational approach to the over-all problem.

Take another example from the absurdity which has become our daily life. Automobiles, and their corollary, freeways, are about as unsafe, inefficient, and expensive a mode of transportation as one could possibly devise for a highly urbanized society. They kill 50,000 Americans each year and injure another 200,000. Freeways cover one-seventh of the land surface in Los Angeles County. And smog in big cities makes life problematic for children and other living things. This is to say nothing about the cost in terms of the human nervous system induced by daily traffic jams to and from suburbia. Given the fact that mileage of travel tends to increase at a geometric ratio as mileage of freeways tends to increase at an arithmetic ratio, it is possible to assume that at some point in the future all automobile traffic in the country will come to a grinding halt. (A notion of "inevitable crisis" in capitalist society which, admittedly, bears little relation to the business cycle.)

Additionally, the necessity of maintaining an expanding market for automobiles leads the major corporations involved to design cars which are guaranteed to fall apart in a relatively short period of time. Thus, an automobile worker in the Detroit area is forced to drive to work on jammed freeways in a car which he knows is falling apart because he has to spend forty or more boring hours each week on the assembly line, building in the built-in obsolescence which he then purchases on the market. Furthermore, he may be saving money for the education of a son who will spend four or five years in engineering college learning to design the obsolescence, or may end up working for a Madison Avenue advertising firm which devotes its energies to convincing consumers that, although automobiles may not be much good as transportation, they are excellent penis symbols.

Not only does the automobile worker spend a good portion of his life doing socially counter-productive labor, he must also live with the insecurity which automation creates for him: the fear of losing his job. Little wonder that he reacts out of fear and resentment to the demands and actions of ghettoized black people. He is caught in a social and economic trap which he feels powerless to alter. Whether he recognizes it or not, only the abolition of capitalist relations of production can spring the jaws of that trap.

Returning for a moment from the specifics of advanced capitalist irrationality to a more general formulation of the problem, it is worth looking at Marx's own limited attempt to formulate the problem of the fundamental contradiction of capitalism. In the preface to his *Introduction to the Critique of Political Economy* (1859), Marx stated:

> It is not the consciousness of men that determines their existence, but, on the contrary, their social existence determines their consciousness. At a certain stage of their development,

the material forces of production in society come in conflict with the existing relations of production, or—what is but
a legal expression for the same thing—with the property relations within which they had been at work before. From
forms of development of the forces of production, these relations turn into their fetters. Then comes the period of social
revolution.[2]

It seems quite clear from this passage that for Marx, the
basic contradiction in capitalist society (as in all antago-
nistic forms of social organization) was the conflict between the "material forces of production" and the "relations of production." It has not been readily apparent
what Marx meant by these terms.

The development of advanced neocapitalist society puts
the problem in a new light and begins to create a framework for understanding the sense of Marx's insight. For
Marx the fundamental trait of the capitalist system of
production lay in its transformation of all social and economic relationships into relationships based on money.
Like all ruling classes, the modern capitalist bourgeoisie
functioned as the appropriator and utilizer of the economic surplus produced by the society which it con-
trolled. What characterized the capitalist ruling class and
set it off from all other prior ruling classes was the way in
which it appropriated and used (the mode of utilization)
the economic surplus. Whereas the ruling classes of the
ancient and feudal worlds had used the appropriated economic surplus to run and expand their empires, the capitalist ruling class used the surplus to expand the means of
production in the societies over which they ruled. This
transformation of the surplus into *capital* was what made
the modern bourgeoisie the most "progressive" ruling class
in all of human history. But at the same time, the creation
of the modern system of production based on capitalist re-

lations of production was a trap; that is, it involved a fundamental contradiction. That trap, that contradiction, grew out of the very nature of the way in which capitalists appropriated the surplus. Prior ruling classes had appropriated the surplus most generally through systems of taxation (either in money or in kind). But capitalists appropriated the surplus by transforming labor into wage-labor, that is, into a commodity which workers were forced to sell on the open market. In addition, capitalists transformed all social relationships (not just their relationship with their workers) into commodity relationships, that is, relationships based on money and the market. This meant that all consumer relationships were also transformed into commodity relationships—based on money and the market. The result: in order to work, the worker has to sell his labor as a commodity; in order to consume, the worker has to buy his products as commodities. No work: no consumption.

That system may have produced an increasingly dehumanized and alienated society with all kinds of brutality and inhumanity, but it seemed to make a good deal of sense as long as the capitalists were involved in building up the productive forces of the economy. But what happens when that period of building-up (the period of primitive capital accumulation) is finished? What happens when the productive forces which the capitalists have organized begin to exceed the primitive needs which the system is designed to satisfy? What happens when the development of advanced technology brings a higher and higher rate of per capita productivity?

What happens is quite simple—and exceedingly explosive. On the one hand, human labor (manpower) becomes increasingly peripheral to the productive power of machines. On the other hand, human labor becomes increasingly utilized for nonproductive ends. And, increasingly for the capitalists, the problem is no longer a problem of how to produce more, but of how to dispose of what is produced. This is where the "fundamental contradiction" begins to produce serious difficulties; this is the point at which the "social relations of production" become a serious barrier to the "material forces of production" which capitalism has created. This is where the absurdity of the "eggs-gasoline-riots" situation begins to emerge.

The fundamental contradiction in capitalism can be expressed as follows: it is the contradiction between the productive capacity (the material forces of production) and the necessity to extract a profit from production (based on the social relations of production, private ownership of capital and wage labor). Capitalism creates a productive potential which is capable of transcending the problem of scarcity, but, in order to maintain the profit system (or, rather, the system of appropriation of surplus value) it maintains the economy of scarcity. Although it is capable of producing abundance for all, the necessity of realizing a profit prevents it from either utilizing its full productive capacity or from a rational distribution of what it does produce. Capitalism has thus entered a phase (neocapitalism) where it is increasingly faced with the necessity of the expansion of the market in order to survive, in order to distribute (profitably) its excess surplus. Yet, it cannot expand its market by producing for the unemployed poor—that would not yield a profit.

In its simplest terms, the contradiction of advanced capitalism is expressed as the *necessity for the maintenance of the work-income connection*. In order to extract a profit, capitalism must maintain both sides of the market mechanism—wages for labor and prices for goods. It is not simply a matter of having to work in order to consume. One must work for wages (less than the value of the product produced) in order to have money to buy goods at a price which yields profits. Without money and the market mechanism, there is no capitalist system of profit accumulation and the economy would operate for human need (use-value) rather than for profit (exchange-value). The absolute necessity for the conversion of use value into exchange value (and the conversion of all relationships into relationships based on money) remains the fundamental characteristic of capitalist production. Break the work-income connection, and you will have destroyed the capitalist system—but that will not happen without the revolutionary transformation of the social relations of production.

In an underdeveloped or developing capitalism, the full weight of this contradiction is by no means apparent. Workers in such a system produce generally useful products and are paid subsistence wages for their labor time. Capitalists extract a surplus, part of which is reinvested in plant and machinery (either for expansion or to replace worn-out plant). At this level of development, the contradictory nature of capitalism seems to center either in its inhuman organization of labor (the ghastly abuses of the early factories and mines) or in the inequitable distribution of wealth (the capitalists get fat while the workers starve). Under advanced neocapitalism, the real nature of the contradiction exposes itself in full force. Once scarcity is no longer the central focus, and once primitive capital accumulation has produced self-generating technological development, the full implication of the work-income connection is revealed as the very heart of capitalist society.

A primitive example of this phenomenon can be supplied from the agricultural sector of the economy. It is clear that the mechanization of agriculture in the United

States has created a productive potential which far exceeds the needs of the American people. Yet, millions of poor people go hungry in this country. In order to maintain the high profits in agriculture which are the result of its capitalist nature (and which do not accrue for the most part to people who work the land), high food prices are maintained through the enforced limitation of production; land is taken out of cultivation (soil bank program) and sometimes produce is destroyed. Why not give it away?—the naïve observer asks again. You cannot give commodities away, for that would undermine the whole system of private ownership and the market mechanism!—the capitalist apologist is forced to reply. Even common sense is struck by the absurdity of this proposition.

It is at least clear from this example that although capitalist agriculture is capable of producing all that we need to eat, capitalism is incapable of transcending the realm of scarcity regarding the question of human nourishment. Thus the potential for post-scarcity which capitalism creates remains permanently unrealized as long as capitalist relations are maintained. The irrationality of such a system was apparent to many millions of hungry Americans during the Great Depression of the 1930s. While many went without food because there were no jobs whereby they could earn the wages necessary to subsist, the government was exhorting the farmers to "kill and plow under" in order to prevent the production of a "surplus" which would keep agricultural prices down—a highly irrational and inhuman solution to the problem of abundance. The only real solution would have involved the destruction of those "social relations of production" which fettered the "material forces of production"—but that is precisely what the neocapitalist regime of Roosevelt was determined to prevent.

In our present situation, the ghettoized poor (who are poor because the economy does not provide jobs for them —not because the economy does not provide enough material goods for their needs) are in precisely the same situation as the unemployed masses of the 1930s. There is one important difference, however. Because they have not been part of the industrial productive process, they are less likely than the workers of the 1930s to understand that their situation is rooted in the problems of the capitalist system. That is why, although they have become a highly militant and insurrectionary force, they have not become a force for socialist revolution.

This example from agriculture is easily understandable because agriculture is a productive category which corresponds to easily understood human needs; furthermore, the potential for post-scarcity in the realm of food is readily grasped. Agriculture is also dependent on a fairly large number of disorganized small producers (in comparison with monopolized and oligopolized industrial production) and therefore has required a higher degree of governmental intervention than other sectors of the economy. Of course, the very same contradictory mechanisms operate in all sectors of the economy. But, the relationships between the State and the giant corporations are more subtle and have remained less blatantly exposed to public scrutiny.

The problem is much broader than food. Children in the ghetto are also without necessary shoes and clothing in an economy which spends millions of dollars on advertising designed to promote fads which encourage people to throw away their entire wardrobe every six months. But, because of the work-income necessity, ghetto children remain unclothed while plant and machinery remain idle or produce garbage. What's more, the fathers of ghetto children cannot find jobs because the economy does not need their labor. The machines could produce the goods—but he who would consume without working does not promote the necessary capitalist accumulation of profit.

There is only one logical deduction which any sensible person can make: the system which is based on profit accumulation is obsolete and the class which accumulates the profits is obsolete. Both the class and their system no longer serve a useful historical function: in fact they promote increasing absurdity and inhumanity in our lives when freedom from both scarcity and from alienated labor are possible. As the American historian William Appleman Williams has expressed it:

> The crisis created by cybernated production is *the* crisis of capitalism as defined by Marx. The capitalist system has in cybernated production fulfilled its promise and potential, and has created the absolute necessity to transcend its inability to cope with its own success. But capitalist leadership literally does not know—it cannot conceive—what to do at this magnificent turning point in human history that was so accurately foreseen by Karl Marx. If left to its limited devices and cramped imagination, the turn will not be made.[3]

The New Demands

Too often in the past, the question of social revolution was presented in the guise of a vengeful expropriation of the rich by the exploited. The have-nots would seize the wealth of the haves. This was the image conveyed by Proudhon's dictum "Property is theft!" It is a notion which makes some sense in the context of early industrialization and the reactions of an artisanry which finds itself face to face with proletarianization. It is, however, a naïve and primitive model of revolution which ignores the fact that real wealth is social wealth. It is not the "riches" of the "wealthy" which constitute the real wealth of an advanced industrial society but the enormous productive capacity of the society as a whole. The capitalist governing class is a historically reactionary force, not because it lives better or consumes more commodities, but because its power over society through control of the means of production prevents the realization of the historical potential for liberation which exists. The capitalist class is opposed not because it is "better off" but because it enslaves us in a system of commodity production and commodity consumption and is willing to resort to force and violence in order to maintain its control over production, resources, and markets.

The revolutionary transformation of capitalist society is not a question of "soaking the rich." It is rather the question of the transformation of a social system and social structures, of depriving those who have power of their control over social wealth in order that we may create a free society and contribute to the creation of a free world. When the New Left talks of transforming the relationships of power, it does not conceive of re-establishing the system of domination with a new form of dominative power. That kind of power is of no human interest and of no human use. Rather, the drive is aimed at the transformation of a system in which "power" is equivalent to "domination" and the creation of a society in which power becomes the ability of all men to realize their creative and productive potential as human beings in a common and collective effort. To reiterate, the major objection to the capitalist class and the capitalist system is not the "things" possessed by a few, but the fact that capitalism is a power over our lives which forces us to do wasteful and meaningless things when we want to do something radically different and marvelously new.

A key factor in the understanding of every period of human social and economic development is the "size and mode of utilization of the economic surplus." The key relationship (the social relations of production) in every socioeconomic configuration is based on the system of appropriation of that economic surplus. Thus, these social relations of production are the *class relationships* of every society and the *ruling class* in a given society is quite simply that group which determines the use of the economic surplus through its control of the means of production and exchange.

The historically progressive character of the capitalist class as the new ruling class in modern history grew out of the specific capitalist mode of utilization of the economic surplus. By sweeping aside the medieval order and instituting the total reorganization of production on the basis of wage labor, the capitalist class was able not only to increase the economic surplus but also to revolutionize the means of production through the investment of accumulated capital in the creation of modern industry. The industrial revolution, the greatest achievement of capitalist organization, gave rise first to the steady and rapid increase in per capita productivity. Secondly, it created an advanced technology, cybernated production, under which production is decreasingly tied to human labor power and increasingly the outgrowth of the application of scientific problem-solving. In so doing, the capitalist class has fulfilled its historic role and set the stage for a new era in human history.

The real challenge which the New Left can present in the midst of mature capitalism is based on precisely these issues. Its long-range potential lies in a struggle against the repressive uses of productive power, and for a new social order in which the liberating potential of post-scarcity can be realized. The New Left is the historical embryo of a new society in which men would be free from alienated labor and the restraints of repressive civilization and able to create a new culture of freedom on the basis of new human relationships and values.

Capitalism cannot create those new values nor can it realize the potential of post-scarcity. It is trapped within its own dynamic and must maintain the "upward spiral" of increasing production and increasing individual consumption. It has created the conditions in which human labor becomes increasingly superfluous and yet it cannot free human energy from alienated work. It has created "surplus labor" but it cannot create a free society. Marx seemed to sense the nature of this development and the contradictions which it contained:

> The great historic role of capital is the creation of surplus labor, labor which is superfluous from the standpoint of mere use value, mere subsistence. Its historic role is fulfilled as soon as (on the one hand) the level of needs has been developed to the degree where surplus labor in addition to necessary subsistence has itself become a general need which manifests itself in individual needs, and (on the other hand) when the strict discipline of capital has schooled successive generations in industriousness and this quality has become their general property, and (finally) when the development of the productive powers of labor, which capital, with its unlimited urge to accumulate and to realize, has constantly spurred on, have ripened to the point where the possession and maintenance of societal wealth require no more than a diminished amount of labor-time, where the laboring society relates to the process of its progressive reproduction and constantly greater reproduction in a scientific manner, where, that is, human labor which can be replaced by the labor of things has ceased.[4]

It is only at this advanced stage of development that the contradiction between the economic potential and the way in which it is used and perverted emerges with full force. The frustration of that potential by capitalist structures gives rise to the new forms of social revolt in advanced capitalism and provides the social basis for the emergence of the New Left.

The changing basis of revolt is only barely perceived but its further development is inevitable. In the period of primitive capital accumulation, the very fact of surplus appropriation was seen as the heart of the capitalist system. In the neocapitalist period, it is not the raw fact of exploitation but rather the mode of utilization of the surplus which comes increasingly under attack. The growing utilization of human and material resources for wasteful and antisocial ends—experienced as oppression both in "work" and "leisure"—becomes the basis for a whole new set of revolutionary demands; post-scarcity, the elimination of alienated labor, a nonrepressive culture. None of these can be achieved without the elimination of production for profit and its corollary, the marketplace, nor without decentralization and grass-roots democracy. Both the economic dynamics and the social relationships of capital must be transformed.

NOTES—CHAPTER 4

1. "The Cities and Revolutionary Organization," by Tom Bell, Bernadine Dohrn, and Steve Halliwell.
2. Karl Marx, Zur Kritik der politischen Ökonomie, quoted in Martin Nicolaus, "The Unknown Marx," *New Left Review*, No. 48, March-April, 1968.
3. William A. Williams, *The Great Evasion*, Chicago, Quadrangle Books, 1964.
4. Marx, *op. cit.*

PART TWO

Practice and the New Left

Note on
Practice and the New Left

The development of a relevant political practice in the New Left has been an ad hoc process, a pragmatic groping toward a theoretical understanding of advanced capitalist society. It began with the same sense of urgency and existential commitment, the same values of community and personal liberation, which have been integral to other aspects of its development. More recently, the movement has become divided and increasingly factionalized over the questions of organizational strategy and political tactics. Rather than engaging in serious debate about these problems, there has been a steady drift in the direction of ideological phrase-mongering as a substitute for serious discussion. There is a widely shared assumption among many New Leftists that there is nothing essentially "new" about their movement and the accompanying tendency to believe that the Leninist models of the Old Left (together with the rhetoric of Chairman Mao's little *Red Book* and the style of Che Guevara) will suffice to provide political direction for a successful revolutionary movement in the advanced capitalist world.

Two political developments have served to reinforce this tendency. First, the national liberation struggle of the Vietnamese has been a major issue leading to the politicization and radicalization of American youth, with the result that their attention has been focused quite naturally on the Third World and anti-imperialist movements. The result has been to adopt the methods of the heroes of guerrilla warfare as the basic strategy and tactics of political work. Secondly, the development of civil rights struggles into a militant black movement in the United States in the 1960s has reinforced this Third World orientation and provided a plausible (though essentially incorrect) view of the black movement as an "internal colony" struggling for its own national liberation within the "mother country." What emerges is a revolutionary perspective which envisions the final triumph of world socialism through a series of guerrilla struggles waged both externally and internally against the capitalist metropolis.

The plausibility of the argument and the élan of its adherents have given it an undeniable momentum—however temporary and potentially disastrous for the future of the New Left. It is essentially the reversion to the catastrophic and apocalyptic view of revolution typical of the Old Left, but it embodies in this new phase an ultramilitancy and adventurism which gives it an aura of excitement which the Old Left rarely had. What is even more striking is that, despite its pretensions to "Marxism-Leninism" and its quotes from Chairman Mao, it is really not a Marxist theory at all. If Marxism is a theory of social change and revolution which attempts to define how the internal contradictions of capitalist society will produce the social negation of capitalism, then it must rest *primarily* on the analysis and understanding of how the forces of negation develop *within* the capitalist social order. Rather than basing themselves on such an analysis, the various Maoist factions talk almost exclusively about social forces which are external or peripheral to the developed neocapitalist world—the forces of preindustrial or precapitalist societies.

It is undoubtedly this inability to come to grips with the problem of how socialism will (to use Marx's phrase) "develop out of the womb of capitalism" which produces the strategic romanticism and the tactical adventurism characteristic of much of the New Left's development in recent months. For, if one cannot identify positive forces of social revolution with neocapitalist society, then one is easily led to believe that militancy in and of itself must be the key which will unlock the future. If one does not feel that the evolving contradictions of the society are creating the basis for social revolution, then there is an understandable tendency to believe that one can create the revolution out of one's own will to have it happen. Isolation, frustration, and the urgency of the international situation combine to produce the politics of combat—as though socialist revolution were primarily a problem of military strategy rather than a question of organizing people around their felt, comprehensible needs.

The greatest tragedy of the present impasse is that the reversion to Leninist forms and Maoist rhetoric has stifled much of the life-affirming content of the New Left and has warped its sense of personal and public values. The return to dogmatic rigidity and life-denying values which colors the present (hopefully transitory) period is indeed unfortunate when one realizes that ever greater numbers of Americans are searching for a meaningful political alternative to both the sterility of their private personal existence and the impotent quadrennial spectacle of the humpty-dumpty politics of the ballot box.

The success or failure of the New Left in the next decade will depend not on its ability to perfect street-fighting techniques, but on its willingness to develop political programs and build alternatives which will involve the vast majority of the American people in a day-by-day struggle for the creation of a new society. It also seems clear that such programs must not revert to the Old Left dichotomy between the personal and the political.

5

The Return of the Repressed

. . . revolution is the conscious liberation of the repressed.
Herbert Marcuse, Eros and Civilization

Perhaps such secrets, the secrets of everyone, were only expressed
when the person laboriously dragged them into the light of the
world, imposed them on the world, and made them a part of the
world's experience. Without this effort, the secret place was merely
a dungeon in which the person perished; without this effort, in-
deed, the entire world would be an uninhabitable darkness . . .
James Baldwin, Another Country

The argument for decentralist and nonauthoritarian forms
is directly related to an interpretation of the nature and
function of cultural oppression in neocapitalist society. If
the New Left is to become a movement for radical transformation in this society, it must come to grips with the
felt needs of millions of Americans and it must recognize
that the majority of people experience the oppression
which is rooted in the neocapitalist economic order as psychological and cultural oppression. The average American

who may have little conscious understanding of the functioning of the political economy which is the basis of his oppression can at least articulate a gut-level comprehension of the society as "organized insanity." The lonely, privatized individual who is the tragic product of this civilization looks out the window of his ticky-tacky house onto the world of freeways, smog, traffic jams, plastic-coated hamburger stands, and prefrozen French fries with catsup.

Faced with the mass culture of compulsive consumption which is part and parcel of advanced capitalist irrationality, the individual longs for *relief*—release from the tension which binds his own life-energy, his Eros, and makes psychic pain the common denominator of his experience with other human beings. Impotent and helpless, he flees this institutionalized psychosis in a thousand individualized ways. Anything from wife-swapping to LSD is acceptable if it provides a temporary escape from the neurotic tension.

This mass neurosis with its hopelessness and despair is the possible breeding ground for mass hysteria and perhaps fascism. It is also potentially the existential stepping stone to a politics of life-affirmation. Unless the New Left meets the challenge of this ambiguity with libertarian and creative politics which permit people to fulfill their need for personal liberation, the positive creation of new community, and the building of new life-affirming institutions, it will end as the fantasy reflection of the existing order rather than as its revolutionary negation.

The repressed content of human existence—the warped potentiality for a human species which is beautiful, creative, self-assured, and productive of life—will inevitably return. The question is whether it will return in its neurotic, sado-masochistic, mass-hallucinatory forms (such as

German Nazism) or in new liberated forms which embody
the new society. When Marcuse argues that "revolution is
the conscious liberation of the repressed" he is challenging
us to build that kind of movement which is self-aware and
intentional about the task which it must confront. We must
be able to move beyond fantasy and self-titillation to the
creation of positive alternatives if we are to tap the immense resources of the basic, rational, instinctual life of
human beings. Otherwise we will only participate in the
activation of their fear and irrationality. We must address
ourselves to the truth of life and felt human need or we
will simply remain another nightmare haunting the dream-
world of the mass unconscious. If, to the public, we can
only offer hateful faces and obscene slogans, raise fists and
chanting demonstrators, then we will be indistinguishable
from the tortured fantasies of that twilight zone which
separates the bourgeois ego from the instinctual self. Unless we become a movement and a people which embody
in their relationships, lives and work the concrete begin-
nings of a new society, then we will miss the opportunity
to relate our own needs and our own humanity to those
millions of fellow creatures in this country who suffer the
same pain, dream the same dreams, and fear the same
nightmares that we do.

It is a difficult task for we have been primarily a "reac-
tive" movement, a movement which has been searching
for its identity, and which, though often tremendously
creative, has feared to trust its own instincts sufficiently to
speak proudly and positively of its longings and its vision.
That, perhaps more than anything else, explains our sloganeering and our posturing—this fear to finally say what
we feel about life. And yet, the knowledge is there. We are
a bit like the psychoanalyst who, having penetrated the
dreams and the false images of the psychic barriers, finds

himself faced with the raw, biological need of his patient, and then, because he is afraid of what it would reveal about himself, turns away from dealing with the final truth. Faced with ourselves, we retreat into the forms of the "old man" fearing to become new. Fearing the immensity of the task of building the new relationships and initiating the new institutions, we style ourselves in the mannerisms and the rhetoric of Lenin, Mao, or Che. Life demands something new: we must be bolder if we are to be part of the new creation.

Socialism and Community

The historic juncture at which we stand in the advanced neocapitalist societies raises an old social question in a new form. For the first time in human history, the search for an end to man's alienation through the establishment of a nonrepressive community and the objective economic-technological possibility for the end of class exploitation coincide in the same historical moment. Post-scarcity and the end of toil (of alienated labor) as the inherent potential of the productive forces of our age combine to make utopianism both socialist and scientific—an objectively realizable possibility and an historical necessity.

There has hitherto existed a tension in radical social theory between two sorts of demands: the demand for man's freedom from economic want and the demand for a nonrepressive pro-community culture. This tension was inherent in the dispute between Marx's "scientific socialism" and the utopian socialist theories which he challenged. At this stage of the debate, Marx posed as an historical "realist," arguing that the transition from capitalism to a higher stage of human civilization will result not from the efforts of small groups of individuals withdrawing from capitalist society to form utopian communities, but from the emergent social forces produced by capitalist development itself. Put crudely, socialism will happen, according to Marx, not because it is morally desirable and desired or because capitalism frustrates man's longing for an end to his alienation from himself, his fellows, and nature, but because the social, economic, and technological organization of capitalist society involves contradictions which will inevitably be resolved through revolution.

At another level of the argument, Marx again vigorously opposed the individualist and immediatist theses of the anarchist movement because he perceived that its viewpoint led in the direction of individual terrorism and adventurism.

Typical of the early New Left was a refusal to accept these dichotomies. There has been an insistence that the struggle for personal liberation from repressive norms, the search for community with one's fellows, and the political-historical struggle against repressive power and exploitation were the same struggle. Nothing has been more heretical in the eyes of "traditional Marxists" than this New Left insistence on the combination of utopian vision, anarchist immediatism, and revolutionary socialist perspective. For it jars the plodding sense of the Old Left and challenges the constipated intellects of the hard-line "dialectical materialists" of the old school. The old orthodoxy has already begun a process of denunciation which will undoubtedly grow more vituperous as the libertarian New Left becomes increasingly self-aware and increasingly able to translate its historical vision into concrete political practice.

The Revolution within the Revolution

Nothing has shocked the perceptions of the general public more profoundly in the last decade than the life-style and cultural forms of the young political activists and their

broader, less political allies in the young cultural movements. Although Hollywood and Madison Avenue have
been quick to turn these new forms of self-expression into
salable commodities, the cultural revolution of the 1960s
remains a revolution within the revolution whose consequences have had a far-reaching effect on broad sectors of
the population.

The elements of the cultural revolution have been fairly
clearly delineated, however unsuccessful their forms have
been in practice. Fundamentally they arise out of the rejection of the mind-body schizophrenia and the aggressive-
passive sexual bipolarity of the established civilization. It
is, however, a common misperception to regard the movement as simply a heightening of genital sexual expression
and a breakdown of the primitive sexual taboos. It is, at
the sexual level, a discovery of the much broader expression of eros and sensuality beyond the requirements of the
"performance principle" of genital expression. True it rests
on a rejection of taboo and repressive structures. It is the
discovery at the psychobiological level that, to use Freud's
phrase, "sexuality is by its nature polymorphous and per-
verse" and rests on a willingness to confront the bisexual
nature of the species. But it is also a positive attempt to
extend the instinctual expressiveness of the human species
into new dimensions of aesthetic and moral experience. In
this dimension, it is very unlike the "sexual revolt" of the
Torrid Twenties for it espouses less the moral neutrality
of "sexual license" than the positive moral content of *nonrepressive community*. Rather than heightening perverted
forms of genital dominativeness, it attempts to rediscover
the sensual entirety of the human organism and its potential extension into the realms of culture and art.

The "unisex" of the youth culture of the 1960s is very
unlike the orgies of the 1920s or the homosexual culture

of the "gay bars" of the 1950s. It is somehow the realization that previous forms of underground culture have been the expression of dominative culture rather than their transcendence. Whereas the cultural revolts of the past, however bizarre, retained the aggressive-passive roles of male-dominated civilization, the new revolt of the 1960s has attempted to transcend these roles and their repressive-historical content by developing new life forms which center around the notion of a community of free men and women. The totality of human relationships, expressed in the notion of community, rather than the abstract notion of individual liberation, becomes the central concern. The cultural revolution is finally not a search for an ahistorical form of individual withdrawal but a striving for new forms of cultural expression. In its most profound sense it involves the concept of the "New Person."

The question is posed for us in a very concrete way: is it possible to oppose authoritarian-dominative bourgeois civilization without turning ourselves into the militant reflection of the repressive and life-denying values which we began by opposing? Is it possible to be something other than the reflection of patriarchal values and still remain an effective force in opposition to capitalism? Is it possible to build a movement on the basis of love, eros, and life-affirmation, or are we condemned to live out the bourgeois values of repression, guilt, self-denial, and self-hatred which are the daily fare of life in this society? The answer seems simple enough: if we cannot transcend the values of repressive civilization in our living and thinking, in our loving and acting, if we cannot develop a revolutionary life-style or mode of behavior—a revolutionary practice—which *transcends* the social norms of bourgeois society, then we cannot make a revolution.

The alternative has already been acted out in the historical role-playing of the 1920s and 1930s. The rise of fascism (in its Italian and German Nazi forms) was directly conditioned by the triumph of state capitalism under Bolshevik leadership in Russia, and the subsequent Stalinization of the international socialist movement. The repressive forms and practice adopted by the Moscow-dominated Third International—including the denunciation of all left-wing elements which did not accept Russian leadership—led, particularly in Germany, to the development of an authoritarian left with a profound resemblance to the authoritarian right. Left-wing(?) Stalinism and right-wing Nazism might well have appeared as equally possible political options for a German working class whose needs were never addressed except in terms of the most repressive-dominative values and practice. If the response of the German Communist Party was to expel all sexual libertarians from the party *as an answer* to Nazism, where were the sexually needful masses of German workers to turn? After all, "smashing the bourgeoisie" and "smashing the Left" are emotionally equal in content. "Which side are you on?" It is, indeed, hard to tell when both sides seem so much the same.

And the question returns: Is there an alternative to being part of the psychotic-repressed right or the psychotic-repressed left? The history of the interwar period offers few positive examples. Surely, the governing classes will always side with right-wing fanaticism (à la Hitler or à la Wallace) in order to maintain their social power and economic interests. Neither do we argue for an alliance with the "progressive liberal bourgeoisie." (Although, we might add, they often seem very conscious of the futility of their power.) Rather, it is an argument for the development of a *relevant* New Left which breaks with the images of the past and refuses to repeat the "farce" of the eternal return—a New Left which has the determination to be part of the creation of a new world by insisting on the necessity of being authentically new.

Black, White, and the New Selfhood

It is important to unravel the themes which have constituted the inner history of the freedom movements of the 1960s. Certainly, in the last decade, there has been no force more dynamic in challenging the assumptions of the "American dream" than the movement of American blacks in search of power and identity. The black challenge to the predominant images of "white selfhood" has been a powerful catalyst in the creation of the New Left. The refusal of blacks to be "niggers" has been part and parcel of the movement which has reaffirmed the values of feeling, desire, and self-expression.

Far beyond political power, which it has largely failed to achieve, the effect of the *revolution of blackness* has been to reshape the potential images of self, of humanness, in the midst of a bourgeois stranglehold on self-expression. Black people confronted an America which seemed both lifeless and obscene—and obscene in its lifelessness. They were the "outsiders" who, though they lacked, for all of their history in America, an effective base of revolutionary power, faced the alternatives of either being "niggers" or "free men." This opposition between the nigger and the free man was like a discordant, erotic theme running through the dominant ideology of "integration." For, everyone else, it seemed, was being "integrated"—integrated into the values and relationships of capitalist civilization. Everyone else was making it up the ladder of the "great American dream." Everyone except the outcasts—those who had been cast out of the mainstream of American life, those who were the bearers of the repressed human content of advancing capitalist civilization. No black man or black woman who mutilated his body or (and) his soul with all the geegaws of repressive self-denial could believe that he was "integrated"—that he had not suffered the brunt of the self-hatred, the life-hatred, of white-dominated capitalist civilization. Caste oppression was at the same time the burden and the hope of black people in the experience of American dominative civilization.

The ambiguity of this situation continues to plague the development of a movement among black people in America at the beginning of the 1970s. Black Power still remains a cultural slogan—a call to cultural alternative—and as such it suffers from the general ambiguity of the black movement. For Black Power in advanced neocapitalist society is largely negative power—the power to rebel, to burn, to disrupt—the power to challenge and to dispel dominant images. It is the power to negate—to say no—without the power to create the new world. Thus there exists the bitter conflict within the black movement between the "cultural black nationalists" and the "revolutionary black nationalists." If one believes with Marx that man's objective social situation determines his place in history, then it is necessary to divest oneself of the existing ideological images of the black movement. Neither group is "objectively" revolutionary. Neither can lead the American revolution. Neither is a vanguard—either for capitalism or for revolution. But both the cultural nationalist and the revolutionary nationalist are powerful catalysts for revolutionary change in America.

We know this could easily be interpreted as another "racist" argument for the "black man's place." That is neither the intention nor the notion of strategy with which we must operate. Every stratum in the complexity of the American social scene has its place—its time and its internal dymanic—whether it be students, new working class, old working class (industrial workers), women, or the disappearing fringe of poor-white farmers. If, however, we are to react and interact in a manner which makes the revolution possible, then we must begin to divest ourselves of phony roles of vanguardism, and begin to invest ourselves with the authentic tasks of human struggle in this society.

To pretend that blackness, in and of itself, is a sufficient cultural basis for revolution in America, or to pretend that it is possible to mount a revolutionary socialist movement on the basis of a minority vanguard, is to indulge the most romanticist of notions. It leads to the white radical worship of black manhood so characteristic of the evolution of the New Left. "Revolution Will Come From a Black Thing" is perhaps its most blatant and obscene expression. Revolution—radical structural change and a new humanness—will not come from any "thing," but from the emergence of human potential and human selfhood which black people will have played a part in catalyzing.

There continues to exist another ambiguity in the black movement. Black selfhood can be defined in terms of typical bourgeois categories—that is, as black manhood. Given the transition from the black patriarchy of the rural south to the black matri-orientation of the ghettoized black north, blackness tends to define its political values in terms of the protectiveness of black men toward black women. The "sons" (who had been called "boys") now achieve their manhood in the traditional categories of maleness. In this sense, it becomes a classical case of the "revolt of the primitive sons" against the "patriarchal father" (in this case white) for the repossession of the women. This ambiguity threatens to destroy the most creative elements within the revolt of the outcasts. American literature reached a high point of cultural self-revelation in the works of the black American novelist, James Baldwin, in the early and mid-1960s. Baldwin's implicitly political statements about the relationships between the sexes and the races in American society dredged up from the American collective unconscious the realization that American manhood had lived for decades in a dream-fantasy world of sexual need and false sexual prowess. White men hanged and castrated black males, not only because they feared them, but also because they desired them. White male America draped itself in white sheets and burned crosses not so much because it detested the souls of black folks but because it wanted to have the souls of black folks. The predominant white American male image of the black man as a beast with enormous genital organs was the product of a white male experience which began with the objectification of his own sexual organs as expressions of capitalist-imperialist-dominativeness and ended with the need for the forbidden—nonrepressed, non-dominative, rational life-instincts—to find their way and their affirmation in the midst of a civilization fraught with repressive taboos.

Women's Liberation—The Revolt of the Eternally Repressed

Particularly during the last two years, there has emerged another current of revolutionary expression and power which challenges not only the assumptions of the male-dominated white left, but the vanguardist notion of the male-dominated black movement also. Women's liberation, as a self-conscious theme in the New Left, grew, interestingly, alongside the emergence of the draft resistance movement stemming from opposition to the war in Vietnam. As a particularly vital aspect of the freedom movement of the 1960s, draft resistance offered a strange paradox: the draft itself was a blatant example of the sexually bipolar values of the society—men were drafted to act out the fantasy and reality of imperialist power and domination. Young men had decided to say "No" to military conscription and in so doing had begun the difficult task of defining for themselves a new self-image, a new manhood. They had to respond to the public namecalling—"dirty, commie, hippie, queer, draft-card burners"—with a new sense of what their own selfhood and manhood meant in opposition to dominative-aggressive values. But (and here entered the ambiguity) what were young women to do in relation to the draft resistance movement? There were some who would inevitably respond by trying to conceive for themselves a role as "women's auxiliaries" to the draft resisters (much as one joins a women's auxiliary to the Veterans of Foreign Wars or the Elks, or becomes a drum majorette as auxiliary to the manhood-proving of the High School football team). Such, however, was not to be the case for the vast majority of women who became politicized in conjunction with the resistance movement. The response was much more direct and more profound.

The emergence of women's liberation as a coherent identity within the movement had been brewing for a long time. Perhaps its first roots were in the early civil rights days, when women were assigned the jobs that mirrored their "place" in the society—as cooks, typists and secretaries for movement men. And, as black power replaced "black and white together," the dialogue was spiced with charges that white women were dedicating their lives to the civil rights movement solely in order to get a black man into bed.

Back on the campus, women encountered the same problems. They found themselves typing stencils, answering telephones, and taking care of the shitwork, while men did "more important" things. Throughout, there existed the pretext that any woman (just like any black person) could "make it" if she tried hard enough. The difference was that this view of black people was considered racist within the movement, but somehow the rule did not apply to women.

The emergence of draft resistance as a focus for activity blew the pretext. It was obviously a man's issue, and women, themselves not subject to the draft, felt uncomfortable about advising others to take risks which they as women, were not subject to. For the first time the alternatives became clear—either be a shitworker for a man's movement or find something else to do. Women found that something else in getting together to organize first themselves and then other women to oppose the forms of oppression specific to women in the society.

Like blacks in general, women suffer a specific form of oppression which makes their role and contribution to the development of a revolutionary perspective crucial. Women also suffer from a form of *caste* oppression. Whatever their class or status, women (like blacks) suffer from oppression which is determined prior to their class position in the society. They have suffered that caste oppression throughout six thousand years of patriarchal civilization. They have suffered it *as women* whether they were black, white, red, brown, or yellow. Their dehumanization is the oldest and most enduring form of dehumanization known in the history of man's-domination-of-man (sic). It is a form of oppression practiced by every race, creed, and nationality of the human species since the establishment of (Engels' title) *"the family, private property, and the state.*" Private property begins—in the language of both Marx and Freud—with property in women.

True, the specifics of women's oppression and the issues of the women's liberation movement are grounded in this period in the particular structure of neocapitalist production. Compulsive consumption makes the housewife the key figure in promoting the garbage-producing-garbage-consuming economy which sustains profits and degrades existence. Nevertheless, the precapitalist ground of the cultural-sexual role remains prior, and overwhelmingly present. Being a woman sold into a harem, or a woman married into the monogamous drudgery (monogamous only for the wife) of bourgeois life, or a woman whose body in a slick advertisement is supposed to provide unconscious motivation for the male's purchase of his penis-symbol sportscar: the forms and functions within each social order may change but the essential quality of women's oppression as sexual objects and domestic slaves has not altered significantly since the dawn of patriarchal society.

All the strains of revolutionary upsurge, all the tendencies within the New Left, bear the mark of partiality which is inevitable inside a social movement which has been unable to define its historical moment and its revolutionary potential. Each runs the danger of missing its historic possibility because of the narrowness of its approach and self-understanding. All the elements of repression will and must emerge as advanced capitalist civilization reaches the limits of its own historical development. Every violation of human integrity and every element of repressed human potential will and must make their indictment of the past and their claim against the present before it is possible to create the movement which will build the future alternative to capitalist society. In the meantime we can and should expect that every attempt at the partial establishment of a revolutionary identity for the new man out of the partial perspectives of each social situation will engender precisely the kinds of tension, factionalism, and heated debate which have characterized the recent history of the New Left. We should expect it, but we must also realize that it is a symptom of our partiality, our incompleteness. Though we have spoken of ourselves as "the movement" we have been and will continue to be for an undetermined period of time *many movements,* many partial attempts to find ourselves and the final roots of our oppression in this society. It is a painful, and often tragic process in which some live and some die—some want to die because the pain of living and the burdens of the past which lay upon their minds and bodies are too much for them. Perhaps all of us, all of this generation of the New Left, will die or be broken because the "objective conditions" were not ripe yet. One can calculate, one can write books, but can one know? And, if not, what are the guidelines to being a revolutionary person without the certainty of success and without the repressive desire for martyrdom?

It seems to us that hope defines itself in terms of both present and future. That, if we cannot know for certain how long before capitalism is finally replaced by a free world and a new humanity, then there is an obligation to work daily for the incorporation of as much of that vision of freedom as one can grasp within the life one lives and the struggle in which one engages. Far better to be defeated fighting for what one believes to be true and necessary and to leave an example of the integrity of one's hope and vision than to opt for some lesser expedient which, after defeat, will leave only discouragement, fear, and bitterness. Far better to have been a Wobblie fighting for the democratic and libertarian ideals of workers' control—and to have lived those ideals in everyday life—than to have been a Stalinist who bowed his head to Moscow control and lost sight of his own ideals.

What does it profit a man if he gain the whole world and lose his own self?

Love, Hate, and Revolution

For many the preceding arguments may seem naïve. The commonest reply to a political position which argues for a life-affirming movement based on nonrepressive libertarian values and practice is that the repressive nature of the enemy and the brutality of his power necessarily engenders a response in kind—that there is no other way to confront power and win. Given the repressive power of the bourgeois state apparatus, so the argument goes, we must become strong in the ways that they (the governing classes) are strong or we will be beaten. The result is to produce a movement which talks about "getting tough," which calls cops "pigs," and which begins to deal with dissenting viewpoints within its own ranks through physical violence. The "battle" is joined and the values and practice of humanness give way to rhetorical militancy and the attitudes of violence and hatred.

It is easy to accept the inevitability of those arguments —much easier than asking if alternatives exist. It is much harder to recognize that an alternative must exist if the New Left is to develop an authentic negation of capitalist civilization. Most disturbing about the transformation which seems to occur within the movement as a result of its reversion to repressive values is the adoption of a kind of unimaginative despair which narrows vision, relies increasingly on mechanical slogans, and develops a paranoid

Manicheaen world-view which feeds fear and hatred rather than building courage and love. The engagement of battle with an enemy seems to imply two things: the clear and definitive identification of that enemy and the ability to muster and sustain those necessary material and psychological resources for inflicting defeat. The solution seems simple enough: the enemy is the capitalist ruling class and we must sustain ourselves by mustering our hatred of that enemy. The resultant logic for the movement is equally simple: we must organize in such a way as to clearly identify the enemy and we must teach people to hate the enemy. The logic is clear enough—except if one does not believe it is possible to build a revolutionary movement on hatred. It is a logic which should deeply disturb all of those who believe that the values which we hope to establish are integral to our experience as New Leftists. We cherish love, openness, and community and want to build a new world in which love, openness, and community are at the center of social concern. We believe that the good society can only be measured by the quality of individual lives and the quality of human relationships and we want a revolution which establishes those values as primary.

Since the logic set in motion by our encounter with "the enemy" is contrary to our values, we feel forced to ask ourselves whether a movement built on hatred can create a revolutionary world built on love. At this point the debate breaks into two camps, one of which talks about hating the enemy while the other talks about learning to love—neither addresses itself to the central question and the contradiction which it seems to entail.

Let us review for a moment our experience of building a movement in the brief history of the New Left. What we discovered about the society was that people were both alienated and isolated from each other. We said that politics was about bringing people out of isolation and into community. We discovered that political work consisted mainly in getting people together so they could discover that their alienation was based outside themselves—in the capitalist system of exploitation and oppression—and that their isolation could be overcome by discovering that they had the same problems and the same dreams and yearnings about overcoming those problems in a different kind of world.

In reality these two phenomena were intimately related. Creating a movement meant building a community in which people could trust each other and love each other enough to be able to carry on a collective fight. Most of our work consisted in building that trust, in breaking down the barriers which isolated people from each other. We can't recall a single experience from those early years of the movement which consisted in trying to "get people to hate the enemy." That is not to say that people didn't want to fight. In fact, the urge to confront the enemy on radical issues and either force him to back down or to act repressively in the face of our determination was an integral and central dynamic of all our experience. What was different, however, was the concentration of our values in our own midst and the preservation and cultivation of those values in the midst of the fight. There was another aspect, inculcated by the radical pacifists, which involved our psychological stance towards the enemy, and there is where the confusion still lies. The pacifist argument was based primarily on the notion of "redemption"— the conviction that all people, even those involved in the vicious or unjust or exploitive exercise of power, can be brought over to our side and made to abandon their present position. We did not feel it was either necessary or wise to teach people in the movement to hate the enemy— we simply taught them to oppose with the most resolute determination the evil and injustice which the enemy did.

The problem with this approach was that some of those who preached it were not radicals or revolutionaries at all —they were liberals. And, unfortunately, it was these liberal pacifists who had the most prestige and the most control in the movement. As a result, instead of trying to build a movement of resolute determination aimed at depriving the powerful of their power, they instead sought concessions from the powerful. Instead of trying to build a movement which sought to oppose and defeat unconditionally the capitalist system, they sought reforms within that system.

Unfortunately, when the movement began to break away from its liberal pacifist leadership, it felt the necessity to repudiate everything that had gone with that period of its development. Since Dr. King was a liberal and talked about building a movement based on love, the repudiation of Dr. King's liberalism also meant the repudiation of the talk about love. Since liberalism meant a moral appeal to the conscience of those who ruled the country, then radicalism must mean that all moral arguments and moral imperatives are irrelevant. Since the liberals had preached nonviolence, then the radicals must preach violence. And so on.

The old *liberal* advocates of nonviolence did great damage to the movement because they obscured issues. The movement still lives with the confusion which they created. Let us try to untangle some of that confusion.

In the first place, they were wrong to believe that power in a capitalist society would respond to their moral de-

mands. They were wrong to believe that the enemy could
be redeemed. Power in this society is concentrated in the
hands of a smaller and smaller group of people because of
the nature of an economic system which enforces that concentration. It is not because the men who have power are
evil men. Their acts—which are *evil*—flow from the fact
that they have the power, not from their individual moral
corruption. The only way they could stop doing what they
are doing would be by ceasing to be what they are—capitalists, capitalists' politicians, or capitalists' cops. You cannot be a capitalist without exploiting people (or else competition would run you out of business). You cannot be
a capitalist politician without passing those laws which
protect and promote capitalist interests (or else you
would be a revolutionary). You cannot be a capitalist cop
without protecting capitalist property (or else you would
be fired and someone would be found to replace you). As
a class, capitalists are as much "trapped in the system" as
we are. The only thing they could do would be to cease
being capitalists—which would solve nothing because
each time one capitalist dropped out there would be thousands waiting to take his place and to exercise his power.

The answer, then is not to be found in converting individual capitalists to our cause. The answer is to identify,
isolate, and expose them as a prelude to depriving them
of their power. The way to do this is not by convincing
people that they should hate capitalists, but rather by
breaking down the isolation and separation of the people
who aren't capitalists. That is to say, by building a community which has a different identity and a different set of
values.

At this point, some careful distinctions need to be made.
But, let us begin by stressing a lesson which we learned at
the Pentagon Demonstration (October 21, 1968), while

we were massed on the steps and terraces of the Cathedral
of American Imperialism. Most importantly, we discovered
the vulnerability of power. Most of us had grown up be-
lieving that the American military establishment was om-
nipotent because it had THE BOMB. At the Pentagon it
was exceedingly evident that THE BOMB was of abso-
lutely no use to the generals in defending themselves
against a determined mass of people. They were exceedingly vulnerable. In addition, they were forced to rely on
troops who are people like ourselves and whom we can
organize. While it is true that only three soldiers out of the
thousands present threw down their guns and tried to join
the demonstrators, the lesson was extremely important,
and it scared the generals to death.

The lesson: conscripted soldiers should in all cases be
regarded as potential recruits to the movement, not as allies of the capitalists or their generals.

At another level, there exist conflicting data, namely
with regard to cops. During the May uprising in France,
most of the regular policemen in Paris were regarded as
so unreliable by the de Gaulle government that they had
to rely on the special "security police" to deal with the
demonstrators. At the same time, the experience of the
movement in Chicago was quite different. The cops
seemed more than willing to carry out the most brutal
forms of repressive action against the demonstrators.
However, we must remember that in Chicago the movement made no attempt to incorporate the redemptive
slogan of the Pentagon: "Join us." Instead, a confrontation
with the police was actively solicited. True, Daley was
stupider than the Generals. But the movement did not
even consider the possibility of trying to win the cops over
to our side.

The lesson: it is not clear in what situations hired policemen will be open to subversion by the movement. Certainly, they are different from troops who are conscripted against their own will. Cops are hired to do a dirty job. However, in a society which doesn't provide enough jobs, being a cop is one of the few jobs open to many lower-class working men. We should neither be romantic nor dogmatic about cops. We should remember that many of them are just trying to earn a living and none of them are members of the capitalist class. The danger for the movement lies in confronting the police with militant street tactics which strengthen the repressive state apparatus rather than weaken it. We should neither deceive ourselves about the ease with which cops can be won over nor degenerate into a movement which spends its primary energies fighting cops in the street. We should remember that a political struggle is primarily a psychological battle—one of the precinct stations in Havana fell to the revolutionary forces when a few teenagers ran in and announced that the revolutionary forces had taken power.

It is perhaps useful to say a few words about "guerrilla warfare" and the current romanticism surrounding it in the movement. Guerrilla warfare has been a very effective strategy of revolutionary movements in China, Vietnam, and Cuba. Guerrilla warfare is a technique for building a base of strong support among the peasant masses of non-industrialized or preindustrialized Third World countries. Despite what Chairman Mao says (political power comes from a gun), the primary aspect of guerilla warfare involves a psychological dynamic. That dynamic grows out of the fact that power in colonial societies (or neocolonial societies) is largely based on the outright repressive military force of the ruling group. Most of the peasant population in those societies perceives the source of its oppression in the local capitalist or landlord. But most of the people don't believe that they can do anything about the situation—rebels get shot quickly. The psychological dynamic of guerrilla warfare involves organizing the mass of the people by convincing them that it is possible to mount a counter-force based on guerrilla strategy. The success of the strategy depends on the ability of the guerrillas to win military encounters and to give the mass of the people faith in their military capability.

The power of the guerrilla technique does not, contrary to propaganda, flow from the barrel of a gun—it flows from the success of the technique in creating a movement, a dynamic community of people who will support, protect, and supply the guerrillas. Unless that movement is created, the guerrilla strategy fails.

From a revolutionary point of view, the basic difference between the political situation of the predominantly peasant societies of the Third World and the advanced industrial capitalist societies of Europe and North America is that, in the Third World, political power rests directly on the outright use of naked repressive force. On the other hand, in advanced industrial societies, political power rests on the assent of the mass of people and their identification with the system. Capitalism in advanced industrial societies rules through the subtle and cooptive mechanisms of parliamentary democracy. It rules essentially by pretending that it does not rule at all—by convincing most of the people that they are free and have a choice. It rules by obscuring power and creating the illusion of freedom. It rules by convincing people that their problems are private and personal problems rather than political and social problems. It only rules by outright naked force when it is threatened (or stupid). When it abandons parliamentary democracy and resorts to police rule, it creates fascism.

The strange result of this situation in advanced capitalist society is to produce a society which is largely governed by internalized *mechanisms of control,* plus the *spectacle of electoral democracy.* That is why the question of building a movement in an advanced industrial society is very different from the problems of mounting a guerrilla offensive in a Third World country. That is also why liberals who play the electoral game seem so vicious to American radicals—they only reinforce the facade of democracy maintained by the electoral spectacle and avoid the gut-level issues which reveal the real nature of control and repression in the society. Liberal politics are the source of great despair and frustration among radicals because those politics perpetuate the illusion of democracy and freedom which are the basis of public apathy and public powerlessness.

Let us return to the question of love and hate in the building of an anticapitalist movement. The very fundamental problem encountered by radical organizers in a society like our own is that most people hate themselves. They are alienated and isolated. They have internalized the values and the repressive mechanisms of the class which rules them to the point that they blame themselves for what goes wrong in their lives. And, instead of organizing a movement to transform the objective conditions of their lives they find other outlets, for example, for those who can afford it the local psychiatrist whose job is to "reintegrate" them into the society. Under advanced capitalism, human lives are "privatized" and problems are conceived of as private problems. In such a society it is not surprising that schizophrenia is the disease which puts more people into the hospital beds for longer periods of time than any other malady.

There are two possible responses to the problem. First,

the problem of people's self-hatred might be directed immediately outward—in which case, the psychotic self-hatred of frustrated human beings is turned into psychotic hatred for an (abstracted) ruling class. Secondly, people might be convinced that they shouldn't hate themselves, that their problems are not private problems, that they should create a political community which is determined to deal with the real problems—the problem of those who exercise power as power is always exercised under capitalism.

What difference, one might ask, does it make which approach is used? The answer: It makes a great deal of difference. First, people who just talk about the ruling class and about their hatred of the enemy don't organize movements—they organize dogmatic cults of psychotic individuals who are afraid to deal with themselves. Secondly, only a movement which talks about the unrealized values (the repressed potential) of human lives has been capable of creating and sustaining the kind of political community which can endure.

This is not an argument for "Flower Power." At a panel on "Radicals and Hippies" at the Third Annual Socialist Scholars Conference, Herbert Marcuse had this to say:

> When we speak of Flower Power, there is one very important thing which we must remember. It is that *the only power of flowers is the power in the lives of those people who love them.*

The only power of the New Left is the power of the people who have become involved in the New Left movement and who, because they know that they are not the enemy and because they know who the enemy is, love and trust each other enough to fight together and to say to others that they should "Join us!"

Building a revolutionary movement which carries on an anticapitalist struggle and creates a socialist alternative will not be an easy task in a society whose unfreedom is so intimately a part of the lives of most of the people. It is not just a question of holding hands—it is not a question of running away to utopia and creating the beloved community. It is a fight: but it is not a fight based on hatred. Rather, it is a fight based on the realization of unrealized and frustrated human potential for freedom and creativity.

The Neocapitalist Moment and World Revolution

Many will (and some do already) argue that because the potential for a nonrepressive, post-scarcity society in the neocapitalist world occurs at a time when two-thirds of the world's population lives in preindustrial misery that all this talk of liberation, love, and community is irrelevant to the real problems facing the world revolutionary movement. This line of argument has produced most of the ideological wrangling of the various tendencies which have come to dominate SDS in the past two years.

Let us engage in a bit of revolutionary projection: What would in fact be the world-wide consequences of a libertarian socialist revolution occurring in the United States?

First, there would be the tremendous release of creative human potential within the most advanced neocapitalist nation. This would have as its immediate consequence in the United States of America the release of the human energy from the irrational bonds of waste labor and waste production, for the building of a rational system of decentralized worker-controlled production and the creation of an ecologically sane environment.

Secondly, it would provoke revolutions on a world-wide basis. The Pentagon's military establishment would not only fold as a prop to the domestic economy, but also as a prop to the governing classes of all other countries within the capitalist orbit—whether advanced capitalist or pre-industrial. In addition, it would totally alter the perspectives of those countries, whether industrialized (Russia and Eastern Europe) or preindustrial (China, Korea, Vietnam, and Cuba), which have attempted to build socialism while having to undergo the process of capital accumulation out of a predominantly peasant-based economy.

Thirdly, it would immediately raise the question of the relationship of post-scarcity socialist societies to the economic needs of the preindustrial world. Fundamentally, this would mean finding ways of making the surplus capital and technological resources of the industrialized world available to developing economies without imposing from the outside forms and policies which would warp and manipulate the organic development of these societies in their own progress toward freedom and community. In this regard, it is important to remember that industrialization and economic development are essentially *social* processes. The important factors will remain the quality of life, the question of democratic control, and the development of nonrepressive civilization on a world-wide scale. While the resources of advanced economies must be *available* for aiding in the solution of the problems of preindustrial societies, this availability must at no time imply *control*. In addition, it must be remembered that access to outside resources will be of only secondary importance to developing revolutionary societies: of central importance will be their unhampered access to their own resources, to their own rational self-determination without the fetters of imperialism.

Finally, the questions of coordination, communication,

and administration must be seen in the context of the objectives: decentralized, democratic, popular-based societies which create freedom and community. National and international instrumentalities for dealing with problems must be subordinated to control by the base. The principles of popular democracy (open discussion of all issues and immediate recallability of all representatives) must be maintained. At no time can problems of international administration be allowed to become the basis for the creation of a permanent international bureaucratic caste with a class-interest in its own self-perpetuation. Forms of organization at all levels should relate fluidly and dialectically to the needs of situations as they arise. A world wide nonrepressive community of free people will not arise overnight. It can only be built if the vision and values remain central to the task, and if we are willing to rely on organic development and popular resources in order to achieve the ends.

The neocapitalist moment in world history is full of liberating potential for all of mankind. Only if we allow our imaginations to be as cramped, and our minds as constipated as the classes which govern us, will we fail to grasp the potential which exists.

6

Consciousness and Form

Sitting in an SDS gathering, which had once been a cross between an encounter group and a Quaker meeting, became a hellish agony when intellectualization and parliamentary manipulation had replaced a sharing of experiences and consensus decision-making. The anarchist style of earlier days had, by 1968, been replaced by rigid debates of organized factions who no longer talked about people's feelings and experiences but spoke in the pseudo-scientific language of Marxism-Leninism. It should have been clear to anyone in possession of their instinctual sanity that these Talmudic exchanges, ideological debates, and resolution-passing indicated symptoms of a deep malaise in the body politic of the New Left and were not part of an arena of meaningful confrontation.

New Lefties had lost faith in their immediate perceptions and forgotten how to trust their basic rational instincts. The conjunction of those two words—rational and instincts—speaks more than volumes of epistemology or political economy about the real insights which the New Left brought out of the private world of personal experience onto the historical stage of what is called politics. People's feelings and experiences had become the publicly avowed basis of people's politics; and in the hailstorm of so-called "theory" or "ideological debate" this momentous step forward succumbed to fear, and the New Left regressed to the Old Left's practice of building walls between the personal and the political.

The revival of Marxism and Leninism created a mystification and obscured reality. Because people felt weak and vulnerable, they began to use rhetoric which seemed strong and courageous. It was like a revival meeting with the old tune "I am weak but Thou are strong, Jesus save me from all wrong." But in this case, the Lord had become Marx or Lenin or Mao. We had drifted far from the simple courage of the civil rights anthem, "We Shall Overcome."

The Two Histories

The question of rational-versus-instinctual or mind-versus-biology lies at the basis of much of modern capitalist civilization and its ideological rationalizations. The mind-body dichotomy was institutionalized in the new capitalist forms of ruler-ruled society. Passive-aggressive behavior—the slave-master relationship—was justified in the holy name of science. Empiricism and positivism developed proofs that the modern world was sane and real. Meanwhile, poets sang their songs on street corners, visionaries were shunted into insane asylums now to be called mental hospitals, and —with poetry and madness safely impoverished or incarcerated—bourgeois Reason set forth to rationalize the world.

One of the symptoms of this reinforcement of the mind-body split came in the appearance of two new forms of expressing the perception of human experience: modern history writing which replaced the medieval chronical or court memoirs and the novel (the recounting of personal life-history in the third person). The appearance of these new forms of storytelling is concomitant with the triumph of bourgeois power and bourgeois rationality. It is symptomatic of the development of social schizophrenia, in which individual experience and collective experience are perceived as totally different realms requiring totally different modes of presentation and explication.

Undoing that schizophrenia is the key to the process of making a revolution in the advance capitalist world. Reuniting the personal and the political was the New Left's attempt at transcending the dichotomy of history and the novel by making *history* and *my story* come back together in a politics of experience. Schizophrenia is, as R. D. Laing argues, a perfectly understandable reaction to a schizoid world. The New Left tried to overcome that split in people's lives by re-establishing the unity of the self. When it failed, the schizoid language of Marxism and Leninism was used to fill a gap which experience had been unable, or only partially able to fill.

The current impulse in the New Left regarding the questions of organizational theory and strategy is in the direction of centralist vanguard notions—the creation of a Marxist-Leninist vanguard party. Although the ultimate sources of this trend can only be understood in terms of the larger political configuration of the country, there is also an aspect of the problem which is *internal* to the movement—its theoretical aspect. Unfortunately, this development has not been accompanied by a real debate regarding Leninism. Rather, it seems that disputes have *assumed* Leninist forms to be the natural, inevitable, and healthy outgrowth of a maturing radical movement. That such an assumption and its corollaries are being questioned with increasing incisiveness among the European New Left should, at least, lead us to re-examine the ques-

tion. This is even truer given the fact that Leninist practice
has produced a style of sectarianism within the movement which generates rhetorical and dogmatic namecalling rather than real strategy and organizing, plus a
sense of bitterness and isolation rather than closer com-
radeship and greater solidarity.

The current isolation and frustration of the movement
are the real sources of many of the present responses. At
the present time, there exist three coherent political forces
of revolt, the blacks, the women, and the students. Beyond
that, the Mexican-American national minority has begun
to develop a coherent political identity and the multi-
constituency, antiwar movement is in a transitional period
of disarray. The increasing tendency towards cadre-
building and combat tactics on the part of New Left students reflects both isolation and frustration vis à vis the
white majority of the country, and enthusiastic identification with black militancy at home and the successes of national liberation movements abroad. This configuration
has produced attempts to imitate the militancy of the
blacks, and the strategy and tactics of the national liberation movements. In addition, it has produced an uncritical
acceptance of Leninist theory and practice regarding the
closely related concepts of organizational strategy and
revolutionary consciousness. Finally, the trend has led to a
cataclysmic notion of revolutionary change which differs
only slightly from the mechanical models of the Old Left.

The problem of isolation is not new for the student
movement. What *is* new is the Leninist response to that
fact. And the increasing dogmatism, sectarianism, and adventurism which accompanies these developments. The
dangers of such a response are manifold. In particular, we
run the risk of further isolating ourselves from the mass of
students who are turned off by the rhetorical dogmatism
and the tactical adventurism. The response is finally an

ahistorical one, for it attempts to deal with isolation through tactical gimmicks rather than historical analysis of the long-range trends in neocapitalist development which will produce new forces of revolt and new allies for this fledgling New Left. The situation is not dissimilar from that of the Russian left which, after having failed in its Narodnik period to build a movement among the peasantry by going "to the people," adopted terrorist methods to compensate for its organizing failures. The question for the American New Left is whether it will be able to see beyond its current impasse and transcend its isolation through organizing strategies and programs which actually build a movement that can challenge the capitalist order through involving millions of people in their daily lives in the struggle for transformation.

The "external" determinants of the present responses go far beyond the peculiarities of the American situation. They are, finally, international in character. For instance, the adoption of Maoist rhetoric and models of revolution derives from the success and the attractiveness of Third World struggles. The New Left did not invent Maoism, but rather adopted a rhetoric and analysis which had behind them the prestige of the Chinese revolution and the attraction of the Chinese people. The situation of the New Left is such that it risks committing the errors of the 1930s —when the communist movement adopted wholesale the Leninist world-view and Leninist forms of organization and work with little regard to the crucial differences between Tsarist Russia and advanced western capitalist societies. Internationalism and the solidarity of freedom struggles across national boundaries is a basic postulate of revolutionary socialism—but the CPs of the west have too often acted merely as propaganda fronts ("Friends of the Russian Revolution"), and too rarely as domestic revolutionary organizations. Their failures and finally their counter-revolutionary roles in crisis periods (the Spanish Civil War, the Popular Front in France, the Liberation in 1944, the "May Revolution" in France in 1968) ought to make one search very carefully behind the sloganeering to the facts of historical reality.

The Origins of Leninism

Leninism is a specific interpretation of socialist theory which grew out of the historical dilemma facing the Russian intelligentsia at the beginning of this century. That rather unique social stratum had come to adopt a Marxian socialist framework in the 1880s and 1890s after a generation of intense and highly romantic involvement in Populism and terrorism. But, prior to its adoption of Marxism, it had already adopted a set of intellectual categories which were to shape that particular formulation of socialist practice which Lenin elaborated in "What Is To Be Done?" (1902) and institutionalized in the Bolshevik faction of the Russian Social Democracy. Of central importance was the Russian intelligentsia's notion of the oppositional nature of the relationship between *consciousness* and *spontaneity*. In his key work of 1902, Lenin was to argue that revolutionary socialist consciousness was not and could not be the outgrowth of a people's movement developing on its own. Rather, revolutionary consciousness had to be brought to the people (in this case, the industrial workers) from without. Left to its own devices (its "spontaneity") the working class would only develop reformist, "trade union" consciousness and would never come to a socialist perspective on its own. In a famous passage in "What Is To Be Done?", Lenin lays out his most precise formulation of the problem:

> The history of all countries shows that the working class, exclusively by its own effort, is able to develop only trade union consciousness, i.e., it may itself realize the necessity for com-

bining in unions, for fighting against the employers and for striving to compel the government to pass necessary labor legislation, etc. The theory of socialism, however, grew out of the philosophic, historical, and economic theories that were elaborated by the educated representatives of the propertied classes, the intellectuals. According to their social status, the founders of modern scientific socialism, Marx and Engels, themselves belong to the bourgeois intelligentsia. Similarly, in Russia, the theoretical doctrine of Social Democracy arose quite independently of the spontaneous growth of the labor movement; it arose as a natural and inevitable outcome of the development of ideas among the revolutionary socialist intelligentsia.

Thus, for Lenin, and later for the whole communist movement of the Third International, revolutionary socialist consciousness was not something that the working class would develop organically out of its own struggles but an ideology which must be brought to them from without by a "vanguard party" whose historic role was to be the bearer of a consciousness which the workers themselves could not attain.

Several observations should be made regarding the historical context of this new world-view. First that the schematic opposition between spontaneity and consciousness, although particular in its formulation among the Russian intelligentsia, is quite simply another version of the mind-body dichotomy so common in Western philosophic discourse. Secondly, that this view of consciousness from without is incompatible with an historical world-view (like Marxism) which sees social ideologies as the product of the rise of new classes and not as the idealist product of a "world of the mind." Thirdly, that Leninist doctrine is not the product of the working-class movements but of a stratum of *déclassé* bourgeois and petit-bourgeois elements which are alienated from the dominant social order but unable to make a revolution on their own. It is not surprising in such a situation that this stratum would look elsewhere in the society for social forces potentially sympathetic to its revolutionary aspirations. In this sense, the Leninist movement is historically close to the Jacobin movement during the eighteenth century French Revolution, when an organized party of the lower bourgeoisie looked to the popular revolution in Paris as a social base for its own power. The subsequent history of both revolutions—the use of terror against the left-wing popular elements and the exhaustion of popular forces followed by a counter-revolution—might give one food for thought.

Lenin did not leave aside the question of consciousness even after the Bolshevik-Menshevik split within the party. In 1908 he spent most of the year preparing and writing a philosophic discourse (*Materialism and Empirio-Criticism*) in which he attempts in a rather cumbersome fashion to treat the problem in a technical epistemological framework. Directed against the Positivists and Neo-Kantians within the Social Democracy, the work develops a theory of knowledge which attempts to justify the spontaneity-versus-consciousness dichotomy. What claims to represent a "materialist" view of knowledge and consciousness comes strangely and dangerously close to the Lockean model of the *tabula rasa*. Sensations are images or reflections of things. Reason analyzes and orders these sensations and yields knowledge. Consciousness is thus "from without" in this sense also.

Such a position is radically different from the belief that consciousness is the organic product of man's encounter and interaction with his environment, for it views man as a passive receptor except on the rational level. It disregards the existence of a biological-instinctual *ground* which is "prior" to the cultural and social forms of the existing order and which reacts to the world in a complex but aggressively active fashion and which also reacts *to itself*. Thus, if the world is hostile to the free development of the individual, he reacts by repressing those instincts, desires, needs, and capabilities on which the world has placed taboos. This means that the organism has a prerational "ground" which is not in the least neutral but which must react by either changing the world to fit its needs or by enduring the repression (or sublimation) of those needs. This ground, this eros, is radically different from the *tabula rasa* which Locke (and other mechanistic epistemologists) attempt to describe. The Leninist view of consciousness comes close to the Lockean model and is thus able to justify the (prior) hostility of the Russian *intelligent* to spontaneity. Or, in other terms, the Leninist model remains blind to the role of spontaneous and organic development in a social movement. Consciousness is not the natural and organic outgrowth of social experience and political struggle, but a rational structure which must be imposed (in the form of the disciplined vanguard party) on "spontaneous mass movements" which are themselves incapable of achieving a revolutionary perspective. An intellectual elite, the vanguard party must guide, direct and discipline the spontaneous movement of the masses.

Leninist Practice and Neocapitalism

In the period following the end of World War I and the triumph of the Bolsheviks in Russia, the prestige of Leninism and the model of the vanguard party spread rapidly until the socialist movement was split in virtually every country into its Second International remnants (the Socialist Parties) and the Leninist (communist) parties grouped in the Moscow-led Third International. Certainly, the Socialist Parties had emerged from the conflict badly tarnished by the nationalistic support which both their parliamentary majorities and their rank-and-file had given to bourgeois governments during the war. But, more than anything else, it was the enormous authority enjoyed by Lenin's victorious party which was responsible for the adoption of the Leninist theses and the Leninist model of party organization, and which accounted for the adherence of thousands of new socialist revolutionaries to the "party of a new type."

In practice, Leninism was to find its most successful adaptation in the various models of guerrilla warfare which were developed as political strategies for national liberation movements in the Third World. In the advanced capitalist world, however, Leninist parties have been remarkable for the fact that they have failed consistently for fifty years to turn revolutionary slogan into revolutionary fact. Most surprisingly of all has been the continued adherence of hundreds of thousands of militants in these countries to formulas which are belied by the facts of neocapitalist development. Lenin's "Imperialism" continues to be read as gospel truth although its economic categories are out-of-date by a half-century, and "What is to Be Done?" with its model of "consciousness from without" continues to offer an historical identity to students who actually seem to convince themselves that their objective social role in relation to the industrial proletariat is the same as the Russian intelligentsia's in Tsarist Russia. Even more striking is the adoption of Maoism—the revolutionary theory and practice of the Chinese revolution— by radical students of the advanced capitalist world as an ideology and model for their own struggle.

At the intellectual level, the attraction of Leninism lies

in its ability to reconcile the actuality of reformist struggles and reformist consciousness among the industrial proletariat, with a belief in the historic mission assigned to
that stratum by Marx. The unfortunate result of this schiz-
ophrenic world-view has been a consistent practice among
the Communist Parties of treating the workers as people
who could only be reached around reformist trade union
demands and thus neither responding to workers' initiatives which go beyond those demands, nor attempting to
raise new and more radical demands themselves. Thus the
CPs consistently refuse to agitate around demands like
workers' control, and consistently lead workers down the
rosy path of economic demands in crisis situations. This
was nowhere more clearly demonstrated than in the May-
June 1968 events in France. Despite its revolutionary rhetoric, the French Communist Party showed itself to be no
more revolutionary than the British Labor Party, a party
of avowed bourgeois parliamentary intent. Whereas Lenin
had begun in 1902 by attacking economist practice, his
followers in the advanced capitalist nations have distinguished themselves by adhering strictly to economist
demands.

The model of consciousness-from-without presented by
Lenin leads, in advanced capitalist countries, inevitably to
an elitist, manipulative, and authoritarian practice which
was so characteristic of the Old Left in this country. Its
implications had been clearly foreseen from the beginning
by such revolutionary socialists of the Second International as Rosa Luxembourg. With a deep faith in the ability of the proletariat to develop consciousness on its own,
and recognizing the necessity for organic growth from
below of the movement, Luxembourg was especially harsh
and acute in her perception of the fallacy of a centralist,

authoritarian organization, and the effect it would have on the movement. Whereas Lenin's conception of discipline, based on his fear of spontaneity, was "self-denial" and "self-flagellation," Luxembourg had a totally different conception of the whole problem:

> Lenin seems to demonstrate again that his conception of socialist organization is quite mechanistic. The discipline Lenin has in mind is being implanted in the working class not only by the factory but also by the military and the existing state bureaucracy—by the entire mechanism of the centralized bourgeois state.
>
> We misuse words and we practice self-deception when we apply the same term—discipline—to such dissimilar notions as: (1) the absence of thought and will in a body with a thousand automatically moving hands and legs, and (2), the spontaneous coordination of the conscious, political acts of a body of men. What is there in common between the regulated docility of an oppressed class and the self-discipline and organization of a class struggling for its emancipation?
>
> The self-discipline of the Social Democracy is not merely the replacement of the authority of the bourgeois rulers with the authority of a socialist central committee. The working class will acquire the sense of the new discipline, the freely assumed self-discipline of the Social Democracy, not as a result of the discipline imposed on it by the capitalist state, but by extirpating, to the last root, its old habits of obedience and servility.

This passage points directly to the incompatibility of Leninism with life-affirming and libertarian values which a socialist movement must represent, and with a movement in which individuals develop the self-consciousness and self-reliance which makes them act as part of a determined and clear-headed historical force which develops socialism out of the womb of capitalism.

The disastrous consequences of this Leninist opposition

to libertarian ideals became most apparent in the neocapitalist period when the increasingly totalitarian nature of social control made the powerlessness of the great majority of men a fertile ground for fascist ideology. Fascism offered the *fantasy of power* through obedience, discipline, and the hope of domination as an answer to the *real needs* of impotent men and women. The Leninist parties of the 1930s had no real alternative, for they too were a cult of the leadership principle. Stalinism in the Soviet Union had been accompanied by the reinstitution of laws concerning the sexual taboos and the increased regimentation of the society. Stalinization of the Western Communist parties meant the adoption of the same sexually repressive norms and the expulsion of libertarian elements. The rigid authoritarianism of the Third International could hardly stand as a bulwark against the political and psychic plague which Wilhelm Reich described so well in the "Mass Psychology of Fascism." There was little in concrete daily practice and life-style which distinguished the Stalinist left from the Fascist right.

In the present period, the bankruptcy of Leninist practice has revealed itself in the inability of the Leninists to deal creatively with the life-affirming, libertarian, and creative elements of the youth cultural revolt. Either the search for new life forms and new modes of self-expression is treated as "petit-bourgeois self-indulgence" or is channelled into "hatred of the ruling class." Marcuse is denounced as "cop or cop-out" by the Maoist Progressive Labor Party and black spokesmen greet the struggle of the Women's Liberation Movement against the sexual bipolarity of the society by announcing that the strategic position of women in the movement is in bed. Instead of dealing intelligently, sympathetically, and critically with the creative life-force of young people in search of an alternative culture, the various self-proclaimed vanguards seem to exhibit Freud's analysis of the "eternal return." Street gangs, guns as a symbol of manhood, and calling cops "pigs" are hardly symptoms of a movement which knows its own power and expresses an inability to transcend the repressive values and dominative practice of the neocapitalist rape-fantasy social order.

The Progressive Labor Party's chant at the 1969 SDS national convention—*Fight self, serve the people*—embodies more clearly the politics of self-hatred and life-deferral than any tome written by the apologists of the rising puritan bourgeoisie as they strove to weld together an ideology which would justify economic exploitation and wage-labor in the period of emergent capitalism. Nothing could be further from the spirit of socialist values of liberation and the struggle for the creation of the community of free men. *Not with my life, you don't* and *Resist*—the slogans, however primitive, of the draft resistance movement—were the true mottoes of self-affirmation and self-reliance even if there was no political strategy which could make those demands into an over-all program. Militarization of this society will not be effectively resisted by the training of paramilitary street gangs, nor by the formation of a Red Army.

The best defense against fascism is not arming, but the building of a strong socialist community with a strong and self-reliant base in the population, and the intentional adherence to a libertarian culture and set of values.

Intentionality Versus Voluntarism

History is not made out of the willfulness nor the mystical insights of great men, nor is it a mechanistic interplay of objects in a giant world-machine. It is a process, a dialectical and organic process, in which life emerges in interaction with the environment of this planet. There have always existed in the Marxian socialist movement two opposing and yet complementary tendencies: mechanical determinism and voluntarism. During the last half-century, Leninism has represented the voluntarist pole, and bourgeois reformism the determinist pole. The splitting of the socialist movement into these two tendencies has had its objective ground in the historical fact that the industrial working class of the emergent capitalist order could and had to be integrated into the capitalist schema in order, on the one hand to survive (the life-and-death questions of wages and hours), and on the other hand, because there existed a totally alienated stratum of bourgeois and petit-bourgeois intelligentsia which wanted to make a revolution but could not make it on its own. The Leninist formulation of the problem of spontaneity and consciousness addressed itself perfectly to this historical contradiction: it assigned a revolutionary role to the intelligentsia and thus satisfied their emotional needs and explained away the reformist consciousness of the working class, thus preserving the traditional role which Marxism assigned to it. Unfortunately, it blinded two generations of radical intellectuals to historical reality and reduced socialist thought to a rigid set of doctrinaire and meaningless clichés, while distorting the liberating values which should have remained at the heart of the movement. With the tragic pathos worthy of a Stoic world-view, the New Left, which began with the attempt to restore those values to their central position in historical development, ended the decade of the 1960s in a orgy of self-denial and ideological irrelevance. After ten years of hope and struggle, it risks ending in what Marx called "all the old shit" (his poetic version of "the eternal return"). Indeed, as he says, "the first time is tragedy, the second time farce."

If, in reality, the class and economic analysis of neocapi-

talism which we have sketched corresponds to the historical reality of the society in which we live, then it is reason-
able to expect that the new emergent social forces will develop the historical consciousness which corresponds to
their objective situation. In fact, this seems to be happening despite the unwillingness of the New Left to address
itself to its organic roots in the new working class.

In an article critical of the current direction of the student movement Nicholas Von Hoffman, of the *Washington Post,* writes of the growing revolt among the employees of the Health, Education, and Welfare Department in Washington. In "Employee Power! New Cry in
U.S. Agencies," Von Hoffman reports:

> There's a little document floating around Washington which
> isn't going to get nearly the attention it merits. It's eight pages
> long and it's called "The Condition of the Federal Employee
> and How to Change It."
>
> Written by younger, college-educated people who tend
> to go to work for departments like Health, Education and
> Welfare, it represents a demand for internal, institutional
> change in government which closely parallels what the uni-
> versities are being hit with.

Von Hoffman goes on to point out that the demands
which are arising spontaneously out of these strata of university-trained workers involve the key issues of control
over their jobs and transformation of the content of the
programs in which they are expected to work. In the same
article, he says:

> In Germany and France two major publications have already
> been hit by strikes, the objects of which are not more money,
> but control over the editorial content, the election of editors,
> etc., etc. After having gained a measure of student power it
> is inevitable that this new alumni would graduate to test out
> the idea of employee power.

By comprehending the flow and importance of those objective historical developments the New Left can devise a strategy to break out of its isolation and frustration and forge the necessary organic links to a larger historical development and base in the society from which to challenge the very foundations of capitalist irrationality. It is the kind of situation in which socialists can begin to understand their role as an active, self-conscious, intentional minority, as radical catalysts rather than as a vanguard leadership. The task of organized socialists thus becomes one of "upping the ante" by raising increasingly radical demands rather than waiting faithfully for the cataclysmic crisis while developing the correct ideological line.

Socialism From Below

Beyond the philosophical, economic, and class analysis there lies a question which arises most clearly in the area of strategy. To use other language, the question of alternatives to Leninist bankruptcy is finally a question of alternative models of revolution. If Leninism and its guerrilla warfare projections are clearly unsuited to the problem of making a revolution in advanced capitalist society, what then is the appropriate strategic formulation? We have tried to emphasize throughout, the critical-practical character of our search for relevant revolutionary theory. Let us emphasize again the necessity of relying on the combination of critical perspective and practical activity in order to develop socialist direction which is revolutionary and realistic.

This brings us again to the question of spontaneity and its role in revolutionary development. Having rejected the Leninist model of consciousness and discipline imposed from without, does that leave us with a total reliance on spontaneity? We think not. Rather we envisage a model of revolutionary activity and development which understands that consciousness and organizational form are parts of the process of the embryonic conception of socialism within the womb of capitalist society. Forms and strategies develop as the expression of rather than the imposition upon developing forms of life.

One way of talking about this alternative model of revolutionary development is in terms of the category of "dual power." Dual power refers to those institutions which are popular and mass-based and which come into being when new classes realize their potential for running the society *from below*. The historical examples are numerous, but only inadequately studied: the popular revolutionary "sections" of 1793–94 in France; the Paris Commune of 1871 which gave Marx his first insight into concrete revolutionary development; the workers' councils (soviets) of 1905 and 1917 in Russia which formed the real base of the revolutions; the anarchist communes, farms and army of the Spanish Civil War; the Revolutionary Action Committees of France in the spring of 1968. Something of this notion, however tinged with utopianism, was present in the twin conceptions of "participatory democracy" and "parallel institutions" which formed the key tactical and strategic notions of the New Left in the first half of this decade.

An intelligent conception of dual power is not limited as a category to the experience of the advanced capitalist world. Any realistic appraisal of guerrilla warfare strategies in the peasant-dominated Third World reveals that it is primarily a strategy for the development of dual power —not primarily a strategy for military action to defeat the enemy on the battlefield. Guerrilla warfare uses military confrontation with the enemy in order to catalyze a base, in order to create "liberated zones" in which are constructed the embryonic institutions of the new society.

Guerrilla strategies are also an organic process of building power from the bottom up—national liberation out of the womb of imperialist control.

Obviously, "free space" or "liberated territory" in an advanced, capitalist, highly technologized society does not correspond in the geographic dimension to the Third World model. One of the reasons why Maoism and guerrilla warfare models have attracted so much energy in the United States is because the ghettos—black, brown and white—seem to correspond to such a geographic base. Finally, however, the realization comes that there are no "communities" in this society which are definable in terms of geography apart from those defined by caste and underclass (unemployed) status. Romantic notions about the waging of "urban guerrilla warfare" within the "mother country" can only lead to political disaster and repression. However much Harlem resembles the Algerian quarter of Algiers, America is not Algeria and the revolutionary model which worked (but did not certainly, produce socialism) in a colonial country will not work in the midst of neocapitalist America. The notion of the Red Armies of the Third World converging by land, sea and air on the Pentagon or Wall Street is not only the most misleading of romantic nonsense, a kind of twentieth century Blanquism, but also seems to be the psychological inverse of the anticommunism of the 1950s, with one important difference—this time the American Red Guards will be waiting on the shores of California to welcome the Red Invasion.

The radicals of neocapitalist countries choose these models of guerrilla warfare because of the failure of mass organizing and the failure to create dual power institutions in the 1960s. For a long time the new radicals saw their only possible task as the "radicalization of consciousness." Thus, despite the parallel-institutions notions of the early years, first SNCC and then SDS abandoned their strategies of mass-based organizing in favor of becoming Leninist "cadres," which amounted to being media-oriented agit-prop teams on a nationally televised network. The upshot has been a great deal of radicalized consciousness and the same old powerlessness—plus the fantasies of guerrilla warfare and vanguard organizations. This time the "tragedy" and the "farce" involve not only the martyrdom of scores of young activists, but the potential bankruptcy of a decade of political struggle in the eyes of an otherwise increasingly sympathetic population. By taking a fantasist step into the style and rhetoric of Third World struggles, the New Left has abandoned its primary responsibility—taking a political step into America.

Either one understands rationally that the objective conditions for revolution are maturing in neocapitalist civilization and one decides to deal realistically with those forces and potentialities, or one continues to play a game of romantic identification with Third World revolution. The final danger is that in the imitative posturing about guerrilla struggle, the Leninist-Maoist cadres will provoke the fascist reaction which will make all rational solutions unrealizable. Until a model of realistic revolutionary possibility is developed by the New Left, we can only expect more repression, more reaction, and more generalized political confusion.

In the end, the dichotomy between "consciousness" and "spontaneity" cripples the very growth of the movement it tries to build through its "vanguard." Especially in these times of expertise, technical jargon and credibility gaps, the search must be for a way out of the maze and into forms of self-expression and confidence in one's own ability to comprehend the real world. It is a search for knowledge, not as power over others, but as a means to power over one's own life.

If a movement is to grow—if it is to be the sort of community which speaks to the needs of people for a better, saner world—then it cannot substitute its own forms of expertise for those of the rulers. It cannot say "You have to be able to quote Marx/Lenin/Mao before we'll take you seriously" unless it is comfortable with the values behind the argument: "You cannot criticize the Vietnam War because you are not Melvin Laird or General Abrams and you don't know all the facts."

One of the most important ways that a movement can help people find a way out of their isolation and alienation is to provide the means for them to express what they *feel*. Unless that happens, unless people are able to integrate their feelings and experience and find ways to build community together, then one form of alienation is simply substituted for another. The movement becomes a mirror image of the society, where people are excluded from the action because they don't know the "right" words; because they don't have the expertise.

There was a time in the New Left when people were listened to because they talked about their *experiences* and what they had learned from them. Anyone who tried to launch into a long, abstract speech was asked how that related to his or her concrete experience, and if no answer to that question was forthcoming, the speech-maker was politely disregarded. During the 1966 SDS Convention in Clear Lake, Iowa, a group of young people came from a nearby small town, with the intention of throwing rocks and bottles at the "communists." They arrived at the convention hall during a particularly dull session of debate over agenda, and a good portion of the delegates inside, mostly from what was known as the "Prairie Power-Texas Anarchist Caucus," left the hall to go talk to the visitors. The remaining delegates shouted that "important political decisions" were being made and berated those who were leaving for their lack of seriousness. On the way out, someone replied, "Talking to these people *is* politics, *not* debating about a lot of paper resolutions." The kids who had come to beat up the freaks stayed for several hours, and left wanting to know more, wanting to start an SDS chapter in their town.

7

One Last Chance

The present period reveals a strange paradox in the political development of the United States. On the one hand, the left is more divided, factionalized, and isolated than at any time since the late 1950s. On the other hand, that force which had created a stable coalition for almost four decades—New Deal, neocapitalist liberalism—is in very serious trouble. Ordinarily, it is the increasing exhaustion of liberalism's ability to provide answers to the most pressing social and economic problems of the neocapitalist order which creates a political opening for the radical left. It is an unfortunate tragedy that while the society is becoming more and more open to a radical political perspective, the New Left has entered a phase of self-isolation and paranoid withdrawal. The result is a political vacuum which is full of dangers as well as hope: hope—if the New Left can find its way to a political perspective relevant to the increasing numbers of alienated Americans; dangers —if the vacuum becomes despair and is eventually filled with the rise of a new right-wing, neofascist movement. In assessing radical prospects for the future, we would do well to examine these developments in greater detail.

The Crisis of Liberalism

A great deal of attention has been squandered of late on the tragedy of the youngest member of the Kennedy clan. Many liberals are tempted to see in the broken career of one man the crisis of liberal politics itself. In this case, as in many others, there is a tendency to mistake the symbol for the larger political reality—a neat psychological trick which allows liberals to put the blame on accidents of history rather than understanding the deeper, more long-range historical trend of which personal tragedies are only a small, however dramatic, part.

If the liberal steamship is about to go down on the choppy sea of American bourgeois politics, then we must seek its causes in something more profound than the iceberg-tip which has rent a new hole in its hull. At least six-sevenths of the cause lies below the surface of those events which grace the daily headlines of the liberal press, and the collision-course which finally seems to be culminating in a series of disasters has been set by currents (historical currents) which run long and deep.

What, then, is the historical crisis of American liberalism? Where do its roots lie? Is it long-range and irreversible? What does it portend for both liberals and the radical left as well as for the right wing? Basically the crisis of modern American liberalism involves the disintegration of a political coalition. It is the break-up of the social basis of the political program which made liberalism a ruling coalition for almost forty years.

From the New Deal to the Fair Deal and on through the New Frontier, the genius of liberal rule rested on the ability of the most enlightened wing of the establishment to ally itself with the popular masses of poor and working-class people through a political program which dealt creatively with the social-economic problems of developed capitalist society. These "neocapitalist reforms" (see chapter 3) were a specific response to the stage of development which capitalist societies had begun to enter by the end of World War I, when primitive capital accumulation had been completed and the industrial infrastructure built. Rising per capita productivity in both industry and agriculture meant that the economic scarcity of early industrialization was giving way to the emerging "affluence" of a new era. The inability of laissez faire economic policies to deal with the problem of distribution and unemployment created by this development laid the basis for the collapse of 1929 and the Great Depression which followed.

The neocapitalist era needed new policies to confront the short and long-range crisis. These policies were developed in the New Deal. Call this alternative to laissez faire "welfare statism" or "state capitalism" or "corporate liberalism." Whatever the label, the neocapitalist reforms were a clear and coherent program: state intervention in order to regulate the economy; social security programs to help the unemployed and the poor; government spending to stimulate investment and economic growth; government sponsorship of union organizing and collective bargaining in order to insure that increased productivity would be absorbed by a steadily increasing domestic market.

In order to effect this program, liberal capitalist interests (like FDR) needed a popular electoral base which they found among labor and the poor. It was this coalition which made liberal democrats and liberal republicans the ruling party for most of the ensuing period. There remained, it is true, both a conservative party and a reactionary party. The liberals represented those corporate capitalist interests which increasingly dominated the national and international economic scene—interests which monopolized their own markets and were therefore able and willing to write off new government programs and resultant taxes by price increases in their noncompetitive markets. The "conservative" party (largely the right wing of the Republicans) was based in those regional and local capitalist sectors which still faced the competitive conditions of premonopoly situations and were therefore directly threatened by higher taxes and higher wages. The "reactionary" party rested on the backward ruling strata of the still largely preindustrial Southeast. By combining forces, the conservatives and reactionaries in Congress could back significant liberal reform measures from time to time. But, in general, for an entire generation, corporate liberalism, and neocapitalist reforms with an electoral base in the working class and the poor, remained the governing formula for what, in America, is called "politics."

It has become clear that both the coalition and the programs of the 1930s formulation are falling apart under the influence of a new set of socio-economic conditions and contradictions.

The Crisis of the Sixties

Since 1945, the economic process which had been clear in the 1920s (and been masked or interrupted by fifteen years of depression and war) has been accelerating under the impact of the new technology of automated and cybernated production. Henry Ford's assembly-line revolution of 1910 began to have its full impact in the 1920s. Computers began to revolutionize the industrial world in a major way in the 1950s. We have already discussed (in chapters 2, and 3) some of the economic, social, and political implications of these developments in terms of the rise of a New Left. Let us now discuss them from the standpoint of the crisis of liberalism.

First, there is contained within this "Third Industrial
Revolution" of cybernated production an increasing threat
to the position of organized labor. Those blue-collar strata
which benefited most from the collective bargaining arrangement of the Roosevelt administration have faced, for
the last fifteen years, the possible disappearance of their
jobs at whatever point the capital outlays necessary for automation become less of a concern than the rising costs of
labor. In addition, these strata bear an increasing proportion of the social costs of capitalism through higher taxes.
As a result (and probably much more due to this than to
the celebrated "racism" of the white working class), blue-
collar workers have begun to defect from the liberal coalition of the 1930s in favor of a "new right wing politics" à la
overtly fascist George Wallace. For example, in the 1968
elections, while Wallace and his American Party were opposed by the union bureaucrats who are still tied to the
liberal-labor coalition, rank-and-file unionists defected to
the Wallace camp. The liberal-labor coalition, despite its
immense financial and organizational resources, simply
was unable to pull off its electoral spectacle under the
banner of Hubert Humphrey. In this regard, it is interest-
ing to speculate what the candidacy of Robert Kennedy
would have been able to accomplish, had he lived. Kennedy would not have been able to restore the lib-lab Democratic coalition, for, even in 1960, the Kennedy coalition
leaned much more toward the new coalition of the poor
and the university-trained than in the direction of the blue-
collar whites. The genius of the Kennedys had been their
ability to see the new liberal coalition in these terms. In
this sense they were extraordinarily sensitive to the character of the New Left in the 1960s. They must have hoped
to use the force of the university-trained "new working
class" as the social base for the new liberalism. In any

case, the defection of small but important sectors of the old blue-collar class from the lib-lab coalition, and their potential alliance with rural poor whites under the banner and rhetoric of the American Party, remains indisputable.

The contradictions within this "New Right" are enormous. The style of Wallace grows out of poor-white rural Southern culture. His record on labor in Alabama is abominable. And yet, he can address northern white workers with an 1890s populist rhetoric precisely because of the second major factor in the disintegration of 1930s liberalism.

Secondly, the crisis of liberalism is determined by the revolt of the urban poor. The Roosevelt coalition was based on organized (or organizable) industrial labor in the North plus poor *rural* strata in the South and Midwest. Increasingly, after the Second World War, the poor of America were no longer left on the land—they were forced off the land into the urban ghettos. And, because of both their caste oppression and the backward, preindustrial situation of the Southeast, the rural poor shunted off into the cities were black. Although the emigration of the urban North included large numbers of poor whites, it included overwhelming numbers of poor blacks. The new urban *ghettoized* situation of the rural black poor created a situation in which that class which was least able to make a revolution in the society (because of its peripheral relation to the means of production) was also the class and/or caste most able to disrupt the smooth operation of the society. If there were few levers of political power which would create a potential for the transformation of America, there were, at least, immediate levers of power for the disruption of America. The "politics of burning" may not have created new bases of power in the American urban ghettos but they dramatized the crises of American capitalism to the point that even liberals like those on the Kerner Commission had to admit that America was falling apart. (They failed to recognize, or admit, that America was not "moving towards" but had always been "two nations, one black, the other white.")

A full-blown, Roosevelt-style liberalism would have probably dealt with this new crisis through massive government spending and programs of government intervention in the economy to employ the unemployed. The Kennedy regime tried it briefly, but never faced the real possibility of contradictions between domestic and foreign pacification: contradictions which only emerged fully after the fratricidal fall of 1963 and the advent of the Johnson Administration. The third major factor characterizing and determining the crisis of liberal-labor politics grew out of changes in the structure of the American ruling class itself.

For, thirdly, the crisis of liberalism is determined by the rise of the military-industrial complex. If the crisis of organized labor and the revolt of the urban poor were not in and of themselves sufficient to destroy the 1930s coalition from below, the ambitions and power of new sectors of American capital were ready to threaten the old perspectives from the top down. For, in addition to the Wallace movement and the "politics of burning the ghettos," there was the politics of burning down Southeast Asia. It is now almost trite to repeat that the Roosevelt New Deal did not solve the problems of the Great Depression through government spending until it got involved in the really big government spending of World War II. Nevertheless, that force which built *permanent* sectors of institutionalized power on a new scale in American life, grew out of the "Cold War" and its very hot aftermaths which made the Pentagon a ruling caste unto itself and its allies among the oilmen and armaments manufacturers of the Southwest into the newest stratum of capitalist *parvenus.*

Had the Kennedy "New coalition" of the poor and the university-trained new working class been made to function, it would, at least, have required that the bombing of North Vietnam not happen. Perhaps it would have been possible for Kennedy to send increasing numbers of left-wing intellectuals into the Peace Corps and Vista (as Roosevelt had sent them into WPA projects) and, thus, catalyzed the idealist energy of the student revolt into acceptable, cooptable, liberal channels. Unfortunately for American liberalism, the contracts of the military industrial complex proved too tantalizing for LBJ-and-crowd, and bombing the north and killing off the "gooks" seemed a much more profitable moral crusade. Johnson not only destroyed the "liberal" image of the old coalition, he destroyed its moral cohesiveness. He seemed neither to have understood, nor been able to deal with the changing forces which surrounded his administration. As a result, while Brown & Root made millions off contracts in Vietnam, millions of Americans came to regard their own government as the most brutal and repressive power on the face of this planet. A more calculating representative of the American ruling elite—a Roosevelt, a Kennedy, a Rockefeller—would undoubtedly have done a better job. Even a decadent Roman emperor faced with the revolt of the "barbarians" would have just "built a Hadrian's wall" and held on for another century. But not the Texas oilmen and their military-industrial friends—profits were too large and too quick to pass by. After all, what's the empire when you can make a fast buck. This short-sightedness triggered reaction on a massive scale against the liberal coalition.

Fourthly, American aggression in Vietnam catalyzed the growing alienation of young Americans in the multiversi-

ties and laid the basis for a political movement of the new working class. It would have taken perhaps another decade for the student movement in the United States to break with liberal politics. Certainly the cultural revolution was already there, and the civil rights movement had provided a focus for the direct-action instincts of the turned-off generation. But civil rights actions in the South still rested within the realm of fighting other people's battles. Vietnam, the draft, and university involvement in military research brought the issue back home for America's seven million college students—back home to the very institution in which they lived and worked, and which defined their lives, both present and future. Without Vietnam, the new-style liberalism of the Kennedys might well have contained the revolt of American youth within the acceptable channels of liberal reform and Peace-Corps-style missionary activity—at least for a few more years. The Democratic Convention spectacle in Chicago in 1968 dramatized the dilemma of liberal senility as vividly as could possible be desired. Hubert Horatio Humphrey might well have the imprimatur of the labor bureaucrats —while rank-and-file blue-collar workers defected to Wallace. He certainly did not have the approval or allegiance of the tens of thousands of McCarthy "kids" who were maced and beaten in the streets by the police of the Daley machine. Intelligent liberalism would have recognized the profound error—the deep miscalculation of the balance of social forces in this country.

It is up against the reality of economic change and new social forces of revolt that New Deal liberalism has been pushed. Weighed in the historical balance, corporate liberalism is found sadly in want.

The Crisis of Radicalism

Revolutions do not happen simply because people are exploited or oppressed. Such has been the tragic framework of human life for six millenia. Revolutions happen because something new is possible—because the old forms of human social existence can no longer contain or give meaning to the new substance of human potential. Capitalism will be historically transcended, not because it is exploitative and oppressive or because cops are "pigs," but because it is no longer useful to mankind and must therefore be replaced by radically different structures of human existence. Freedom will not happen because capitalism is a brutal form of class rule, but because freedom is possible. The question of socialism, of an historical alternative, is not a question of material advance but a question of human freedom. Libertarian values are not necessary to the left simply because they are morally desirable but because they express real human need and real posibility and because there is no other way for people to begin to express the potential for a new world outside the incorporation of those values into their daily existence.

The crisis of radicalism is its inability to grasp the revolutionary import of these facts—the inability to see that the first revolutionary instinct is the basic rational desire to live, to be free, to express one's longings and desires in a community of free persons—the desire not to die or be walking-death slaves to someone else's demands and priorities. The basis of revolutionary movement is the instinct to live—Eros—as against the instinct to die (Thanatos.) Unless the left can grasp the revolutionary nature of the basic, rational, life-affirming drives of real people, it will have failed to understand its task.

If the political vacuum of advanced capitalist society is

not filled by a New Left politics which is sincerely "new," then we cannot hope for more than continued frustration and confusion in the body politic. At worst, we can expect that the "new right" which hovers in the wings will fill the vacuum with a fascist upsurge; and, if this is joined by the economic magnates of the military-industrial complex, the establishment of a new form of fascist dictatorship —the political version of the "eternal return"—is possible. If the history of Nazism's rise in Germany has any basic lesson for the left, it is that the struggle of a totalitarian left against a totalitarian right will always end in the victory of fascism. Only if the left can present an authentically libertarian alternative is there any hope.

It would be easy to attribute the failures of the New Left to the moral weakness or evil intentions of diabolical individuals or groups of individuals. The facts of real life force us to look beyond. The failure to comprehend the nature and potential of the historical moment in which we live is neither an intellectual nor a moral failure. It, too, is the product of conditions—objective historical conditions. In order to understand the crisis of radicalism, we must be able to identify those conditions.

Clearly the greatest weakness of the New Left over the past decade has been its failure to consolidate a mass base on the campuses. Until the rise of Leninist vanguardism and the adoption of pseudo-guerrilla tactics, it seemed that SDS might itself evolve into a mass organization of students and faculty rather than the centralist cults into which it has disintegrated. While a decentralist position still carried weight within the organization, such a strategic perspective still seemed possible. The 1966 National Convention of SDS at Clear Lake, Iowa, was presented with a position paper, "Towards Student Syndicalism," which envisaged such a strategy for mass organizing on the campuses. Carl Davidson, author of the paper, identified himself at the time as an anarcho-syndicalist in the tradition of the IWW and was elected National Vice-President at the Convention.

The pull of the antiwar movement and the ideological invasion of SDS by the Maoist Progressive Labor Party diverted the organization from the student syndicalist perspective. Draft resistance and much talk about organizing blue-collar workers left SDS with no real strategy for mass organizing on the campuses. In fact, "student power" or any notion of organizing students and faculty around immediate demands for control in the multiversities came to be regarded as "petit-bourgeois radicalism" designed to protect or enhance the "white-skin privileges" of the "middle-class intelligentsia." The attempt to break this impasse on the theoretical level with the twin analyses of "neocapitalism" and the "new working class" was met with a barrage of quotations from Comrade Lenin and Chairman Mao. Instead of organizing America's seven million students and 500,000 multiversity staff into "one big union" in the grand Wobbly tradition, SDS made a disastrous attempt to organize a few hundred militants into a vanguard party and destroyed itself in the process. Whether that disintegration represents the demise of the New Left or the possibility of a new beginning remains to be seen. Perhaps America will witness the same tragedy which overtook the Japanese New Left in the 1960s, when the student movement split into a dozen or more Leninist factions given over entirely to the tactics of street-fighting with the police or in-fighting amongst themselves.

The effective renewal of the New Left in the 1970s will depend on a number of important factors. First, the development of a program for long-term mass organization on the campuses is a major priority. Unless a radical syndicalist strategy for student-faculty unionism is implemented, the campus base of the movement will sink into deeper and deeper frustration and more absurd forms of adventurism. Such a program must incorporate the basic notions developed by André Gorz of "revolutionary reforms." Those reforms must be both structural and substantive. They must speak to the need for both *control* by the base (students, faculty, and staff) and *transformation* of the content and function of the multiversity.

Secondly, the student movement must drop its elitist vanguardism and develop a model of radical activity which links campus struggles *organically* rather then *mechanically* to other sectors of the society. Student-faculty unions could serve as models of radical mass action and catalysts for the larger society. Rather than fighting around the cooptable wages-and-hours demands which have made "business unionism" the partner of neocapitalist control, they must aim their program in a direction which begins to talk to workers in the organized labor movement about workers' and community control and the transformation of productive resources for human need rather than waste and profit. The multiversity must become a living model of the struggle for a new society. In this regard, the form of such organizations must embody the principle of direct democracy and reject (as the IWW did) the signing of contracts. Labor bureaucracies have operated as cops on the labor movement every time they have signed a contract. All decisions should be reached in mass popular assemblies and implemented by representatives who are immediately recallable by the organization.

Thirdly, the values and life-style of the youth revolt must be articulated in a manner which speaks directly to the potential in our society for the realization of post-scarcity and the creation of the "community of free persons."

Instead of hiding behind the rhetoric of "socialism," communism" or "anarchism," the New Left must begin to make its vision of the liberated human community explicit. Given the exhaustion of socialist rhetoric in the twentieth century, a determined effort must be made to break the language barrier. To every question such as, "What do you mean by socialism or communism or anarchism," radicals must be able to spell out in vision and strategy the content of that notion and the means for its implementation.

Beyond the Campus

Much more important, however, than its discovery of new forms of organization on the campus is the question of New Left organizing beyond the confines of the multiversity system. Current notions among radicals that communities like Berkeley, with its amalgam of "street people" and students represent *liberated zones* analagous to areas of guerrilla struggle in the Third World are not only tactically romantic but strategically self-defeating. Such "zones" could be wiped out in a week (as effectively as in the Dominican Republic) if they began to assume a posture of military confrontation.

Instead of building "anti-pig" consciousness and strategies of urban guerrilla warfare, the left must build organizing drives which are both massive and concrete among precisely those strata which Nixon's New Right regard as their popular base. Furthermore, those organizing strategies must aim at a unity of radical concern which reunites a fragmented people—working people in America, whether new or old working class, whether blue-collar or professional, around the communality of their human interests. Or, to use once again the language of the early New Left, that people should be brought together in order to determine the decisions which affect their lives. It is this basis of the demand for control—community and workers' control—which can be the focus for a new thrust of real rather than rhetorical people's power.

Finally, the New Left must encourage and develop a freedom of experimentation which encourages spontaneity and a self awareness which builds seriousness without authoritarianism. The tragic fragmentation of SDS should serve as a historical lesson in the futility of vanguard centralism and attempts to create the revolution from above.

Needless to say the New Left must rediscover what two youthful comrades in SDS once described as the essential qualities of all radicals: patience and a sense of humor. Without patience, we lose sight of the larger process of becoming of which we are a part. Without humor, we lose sight of the contradictions within ourselves. And, as someone once remarked, without love, we sound like brass cymbals and tinkling bells.

We have, as it were, another chance. It may be our last.

About the Authors

GREG CALVERT is a graduate of the University of Oregon. He also studied at the University of Paris, as a Woodrow Wilson fellow in history, and at Cornell University; from 1964 through 1966, he taught history at Iowa State University. He left the academic world for full-time work with Students for a Democratic Society, serving for a year as its national secretary and writing for its newspaper, *New Left Notes*. Mr. Calvert has been a columnist for *The Guardian* and has written several articles for *Liberation* magazine. He is currently working as a drug addiction specialist in the Illinois State Drug Program.

CAROL NEIMAN is a native of Dallas, Texas. She is the founder of *The Rag*, an underground political newspaper in Austin, Texas. She has worked for SDS since 1966 and served as the editor of *New Left Notes* in 1968. She continues to do radical political work, and several of her articles and columns have appeared in *The Guardian*.